Praises

I0088684

Advanced praises for *Navigating Dual Immersion:*
A Teacher's Companion for the School Year and Beyond

"The information contained in this book is priceless! Valerie brings the unique view of having been a practitioner in the trenches to the more reflective discourse of a researcher. Highly recommended for all new teachers and excellent for those teachers who want to improve and reground their craft."
— Gregg Roberts, Director of Dual Language Studies
American Councils for International Education

"Dr. Sun's book, *Navigating Dual Immersion: A Teacher's Companion for the School Year and Beyond,* is a user-friendly roadmap for teachers entering the world of dual immersion programming. By using personal letters as the vehicle to share information with the reader, the author is able to walk a prospective language educator/advocate from the teaching credentialing and interviewing process all the way through the entire first year of service. The resource will benefit anyone seeking to better serve emergent bilingual and multilingual students in an immersion setting."
— Dr. José Medina, Chief Educational Advocate
Dr. José Medina: Educational Solutions

"It is *avec plaisir* that I offer my highest recommendation for Valerie Sun and her new book, *Navigating Dual Immersion: A Teacher's Companion for the School Year and Beyond*. Valerie's experience as a French immersion teacher in one of the premier language immersion programs in California (Glendale Unified School District) along with her strong educational and linguistic background give her an amazing compendium of knowledge that will be of tremendous help to new and prospective language immersion educators. Her sparkling personality shines through in her letters with important and detailed tips—and the sociocultural touches for success! As we push to provide today's school children with the world-class education they

deserve under our Global California 2030 initiative, Valerie's current contribution will support the recruitment of teachers needed to expand access to and high levels of proficiency in world languages."
— Sarah Rice Fox, CA K-12 Bilingual Educator (Retired)
Certified Trainer for OCDE Project GLAD®

"Navigating Dual Immersion: A Teacher's Companion for the School Year and Beyond is chock full of helpful and heartfelt advice to dual immersion teachers of any target language. It is a practical compilation, in the form of letters and checklists, that is infused with Dr. Sun's own experiences as a former French immersion teacher, observer of other immersion teachers, and collaborator with both fellow immersion teachers and subject-area colleagues. Through the letters and checklists, the author prepares and champions teachers through such events as the first day of school and back to school night and deals with such challenging topics as dealing with parents, assessment in the immersion language, and strategies for teaching special needs students. This book is an extraordinary resource for new immersion teachers and for experienced teacher new to the immersion classroom."
— Dr. Ann Snow, Professor, Charter College of Education
California State University, Los Angeles

"Navigating Dual Immersion: A Teacher's Companion for the School Year and Beyond provides guidance for prospective teachers who are considering a path to teaching in a dual language program, taking them through the complex issues that come up when they walk into their first classroom. Through a series of letters, Dr. Sun tackles things like job interviews, the first day of class, back-to-school night, giving advice on things that new teachers might not even think about before they are confronted with them. She then provides checklists to help teachers get organized. This book will be a valuable addition to any new prospective or new teacher's toolkit. I wish I had this advice when I started out."
— Dr. Sharon H. Ulanoff, Professor, Bilingual/Multicultural and Literacy Education
California State University, Los Angeles

"Whether you are a new teacher to Dual Language Immersion education or a veteran, this guide will facilitate the kind of fun and engaged learning your bilingual and multilingual students need to grow with and through their language(s). She understands the vital importance of cultivating a community of program supporters, starting with our parents who value the language immersion process, the administrators who need to understand the particular needs of a program, and the colleagues with whom we collaborate, whether your program is just starting or is in place. Through her experience of language learning throughout her life, immersion teaching from kindergarten to higher education, content and resource development, teacher coaching and training for effective implementation, and modeling the easy use of educational technologies for purposeful in-person and virtual learning, *Navigating Dual Immersion: A Teacher's Companion for the School Year and Beyond* is a handbook to enjoy reading, to inspire you, and refer to as you grow and develop in exciting ways as a Dual Language immersion professional. Bonne lecture! ¡Buena lectura!"
— Monique Clifford, MA, Teacher
Language Academy, San Diego

"Dual-language education is booming in the United States and around the world with more and more teachers joining and working in bilingual classrooms. Written by a scholar-practitioner gifted with a unique expertise in dual-language education, having worked in Chinese-English, French-English, and Spanish-English dual-language programs, *Navigating Dual Immersion: A Teacher's Companion for the School Year and Beyond* provides much-needed resources and guidance for bilingual educators as they embark in this empowering journey."
— Dr. Fabrice Jaumont, Author, Educator, Advisor at the Embassy of France to the United States

NAVIGATING DUAL IMMERSION

A Teacher's Companion for the School Year and Beyond

Valerie Y. Sun, Ed.D.

TBR Books
New York - Paris

Copyright © 2022 by Valerie Sun

All rights reserved. No part of this publication may be reproduced, distributed, or transmitted in any form or by any means, without prior written permission.

TBR Books is a program of the Center for the Advancement of Languages, Education, and Communities. We publish researchers and practitioners who seek to engage diverse communities on topics related to education, languages, cultural history, and social initiatives.

CALEC - TBR Books
750 Lexington Avenue, 9th floor
New York, NY 10022
USA
www.calec.org | contact@calec.org
www.tbr-books.org | contact@tbr-books.org

ISBN 978-1-63607-222-7 (paperback)

Library of Congress Control Number: 2022933669

DEDICATION

This book is dedicated to my parents who always believed that I am an author and consistently encouraged me to share my ideas with the world.

It is also dedicated to my kindergarten team: Elke, Jill, Laura, and Sonya. I would not have survived without you.

ACKNOWLEDGEMENTS

I would like to thank my parents, Thai and Jersey, for raising me in a multilingual household while instilling a strong sense of pride in our Chinese heritage when we immigrated to the United States. Unknowingly, their support for my decision to study abroad in France also helped pave my career as a dual immersion educator.

My sincerest appreciation goes to my administrators at Franklin Magnet School, Vickie, Ana, and Jessica, who saw my passion for teaching and believed that I was the best candidate to pioneer a French immersion program with the inaugural class even though I am not a native speaker.

The OG kindergarten team, Elke, Jill, Laura, and Sonya, you were and still are my rock. I am so thankful for your unwavering support.

To Fabrice, who told me after reading his book, *The Bilingual Revolution*, that the nitty gritty details of a dual immersion program, the classroom practices, and the relationships with students and parents should be in my voice and my words. Thank you for your encouragement and for providing a platform to share my experience.

Last, and definitely not least, to the parents whose children I had the privilege to teach, thank you for trusting me with your babies. This book would not have been possible without your support of the French program. You provided me with opportunities to experiment with different lessons and classroom practices to find the best strategies to engage your students in their language learning adventure. This book is everything your children have taught me. *Merci, infiniment.*

PREFACE

What's in a name? There was a debate regarding the title of this book. Should "dual immersion" be written as "dual-language immersion?" Would I be alienating a group of academics, educators, or parents by using "dual immersion" instead of "bilingual education"? What about using "two-way immersion" so that the type of language program this book is written for would be more defined?

I sat with the words and spoke to multiple people about the naming convention. The conclusion was to write this preface to explain my choice for naming this series *Navigating Dual Immersion*. In my practice, I use the phrases "dual immersion" and "dual-language immersion" interchangeably. I use the acronyms DI or DLI in professional settings, depending on the audience and the naming convention they use at their school site or district.

That said, I refrained from using "bilingual education" in the naming convention of this series due to its large umbrella and California's educational past. For me, bilingual education refers to a time when educators used the students' native language in class only as a scaffold and the goal was to help students become fluent in English. It was a period when heritage languages were not valued in promotion of fluency in English.

Dual immersion programs generally have a mix of heritage language speakers and English only students who will learn the instructional language. The goal is to help students become proficient in both the instructional language and English. In addition to the teacher, heritage speakers for either language are language models for their peers. This environment values non-English languages and cultures while explicitly promoting the importance in learning both languages.

Thus, my reasons for using the term "dual immersion" for this series.

All of the resources mentioned in this book
can be found on:

empowered-consulting.com/immersion

TABLE OF CONTENTS

LETTER 1: YOUR BIG DECISION

Dear Future Dual Immersion Teacher,

Hoorah, you have decided to become a dual immersion teacher and you have purchased (or borrowed) this book!

The decision to become a teacher, more specifically, a dual immersion teacher, is a big deal. I am so thankful that you have chosen this path because simply stated, we need you. Your love, passion, and desire to connect future leaders with their own cultures as heritage speakers, or to help monolingual children discover a second language and culture is commendable. The road ahead is tough but extremely rewarding. You have made it here and it is now the time to embrace all the adventures ahead!

Here is a hard truth: Those who say, "teaching is easy" are lying. In fact, dual immersion is going to be double the amount of work compared to English only teaching. If you are in this profession for the breaks and vacations, you are in the wrong space. I can guarantee that. As an educator since 2005, I have never worked as hard as I did when I was a kindergarten French immersion teacher. With 17-18 hours of work every day during my first year, I was proud of and satisfied with the curriculum I have created despite the physical and mental fatigue. The language growth of my students and the relationships that I was able to build with them and their families were priceless. These gems continue to carry me through my work today as a community advocate, consultant, and district leader. I know in my heart of hearts that I will always and forever be a kindergarten dual immersion teacher. Please know that the fatigue you will feel will be worth it, as long as your heart is in the right place.

I was lucky to have had the most amazing kindergarten team that I could have ever asked for to guide and support me. Each of us taught a different immersion language: French, Italian, German, and

Spanish and while the languages were different, we had a lot of similar activities and projects in our classrooms. We trusted each other to experiment with all sorts of ideas. My French language team was great, too. We had our differences, but we recognized that our students' learning needed to be at the center of all our decisions. We spent a lot of time together at the beginning of the program to create the alignment that we currently have.

I hope your teams - both language and grade level - are and will be as awesome and enthusiastic as mine. If you happen to be the first teacher of your school's program, please do not worry. Embrace the silver lining of the creative freedom you have and join a professional learning community or network (PLC or PLN) to receive the international support you will need. Remember, you do not ever have to reinvent the wheel; a lot of other teachers have already done the work and are happy and willing to share. You may, however, find yourself spending time editing to make it "yours."

With the craziness in our world and multiple attacks on the teaching profession, I hope that you continue to believe in humanity and the differences you will make as an educator. Our paychecks are small, but they also come in various forms of human capital. There will be tough days ahead where your effort feels futile. Look at the big picture, stay on course, and remember your reason for becoming an educator. I would not trade the impact I have made as an educator for anything. Teaching our future leaders and forming positive relationships with the parents and my peers is my investment in human capital. Randomly, I receive what I call "human capital paychecks" from various people with whom I have crossed paths. These "paychecks" often bring me tears of joy and a sense of pride that I am unable to put into words. I know that if I want to feel like a rockstar, all I have to do is walk on the campus of the school where I was the first teacher of the French program. The kids come rushing in to give me hugs and speak to me in impeccable French. Don't get me wrong, I do wish that teachers were paid more for our work. Furthermore, I feel strongly that dual immersion teachers should receive an extra stipend for the unaccounted invisible work we do. But I digress...

I hope the following letters, written frankly and without fluff, will encourage you throughout your first year of teaching dual immersion. Even though I started my dual immersion journey as an experienced teacher, these were the skills I needed during my first years as an immersion teacher. The topics of these letters were subjects and words that I have said to my mentees at one point or another. In all ways, I hope you find the human capital paychecks worthwhile in this dual immersion adventure. I hope you see the value and gift of multilingualism and curiosity that you are providing for your students as you develop in this profession.

I wish you the very best on this crazy, fun, and challenging adventure. You are a rockstar and you've got this!

Your Cheerleader,

Valerie

LETTER 2: GETTING THE TEACHING CREDENTIAL(S)

Dear Future Dual Immersion Teacher,

YAY! You are here and you are trying to figure out a plan to become a dual immersion teacher. With 42 states and Washington DC participating in the Seal of Biliteracy[1] across the United States, there has been a surge in teaching opportunities. There are similar requirements to become a dual immersion teacher in each state, but this letter is only to serve as a guide. Each state is a little different and you will need to verify specific requirements with your state's department of education. The two most important things to keep in mind are that 1) you will need to be certified as a teacher in your state and 2) you will need to demonstrate proficiency in your instructional language of choice either through courses or exams.

Here is some good news: In recognition of the demand for world language and dual immersion teachers, the powers that be have created multiple pathways for passionate bilinguals to become language educators. There are generally two scenarios to obtain a teaching credential:
1. Traditional Pathway Teachers - You are college bound or a college-age student and you would like to become an educator; or
2. Alternative Pathway Teachers - You are a professional in another field and realize that your joy would be teaching in a dual immersion program.

I will do my best to explain your pathways and list the resources necessary so that you can start your research more easily. It may feel

---

[1] The Seal of Biliteracy is "an award given by a school, school district or county office of education in recognition of students who have studied and attained proficiency in two or more languages by high school graduation." sealofbiliteracy.org/

complicated, or it may feel like a burden, especially if you are in Scenario 2; however, please do not get discouraged by the hurdles. You will find your effort to get certified worthwhile once you are in the classroom with your own set of students. The elation and excitement of having your first class are incomparable!

Scenario 1: Traditional Pathway Teachers
Woohoo, you knew early on that you wanted to be a teacher! Your path should be quite straightforward as you go into college. In many states, like Illinois,[2] Louisiana,[3] and New York,[4] universities offer bachelor degrees in a college of education, where your degree will prepare and lead you toward earning your teaching credentials by the time you graduate. If you have the option to choose to be in a program that focuses on dual immersion, make sure you select that option as there is often an extra certificate that will demonstrate your language and cultural proficiency in the instructional language. During your undergraduate studies, your courses will include student teaching where you gain classroom experience under the tutelage of a mentor who may be a dual immersion teacher. In other states, such as California[5] and Georgia,[6] students can earn a bachelor's degree in any subject and then apply for a one- or two-year state-approved teacher credentialing program to become a certified teacher. In this case, the major you select depends greatly on the grade level you would like to teach. Teacher Certification Degrees[7] is a website that offers comprehensive information for all 50 states and links you to your state's department of education or professional commission.

---

[2] Website for the Illinois State Board of Education: www.isbe.net/licensure
[3] Website for the Louisiana Department of Education:
www.teachlouisiana.net/Prospect.aspx
[4] Website for the New York Department of Education: teachnyc.net/pathways-to-teaching
[5] Website for the California Commission on Teacher Credentialing:
www.ctc.ca.gov/credentials/teach
[6] Website for the Georgia Professional Standards Commission:
www.gapsc.com/ProspectiveEducator/StepsToTeach/Home.aspx
[7] Website for Teacher Certification Degrees: www.teachercertificationdegrees.com

Selecting your school and/or program. I will be honest and acknowledge that teachers' salaries are not very high compared to those of other professionals with whom they share similar educational qualifications, e.g. a bachelor's or master's degree. According to the National Center for Education Statistics,[8] the average teacher salary in the United States is $63,645 for 2019-2020. While there are teacher loan forgiveness programs for teaching in Title I schools to lessen the burden of student loans and a lower salary, state universities may be the most affordable option. Furthermore, Kelly and Northrop[9] found that teachers who attended highly competitive schools "have an 85% greater likelihood of leaving their profession" in the first five years than their peers who attended a less selective school due to perceived teaching expectations versus the reality. Personally, knowing that both an undergraduate degree and a teaching certificate from an Ivy League or a state university would provide the same opportunities, I chose public schools for all of my degrees and teaching certifications. Nevertheless, by all means, select a university that makes you feel welcome and included and make sure that your school of choice has a state recognized and approved program for teacher certification.

Most people know which age group they would like to teach. Even if you would like to keep your options open or see the benefits and delights of all age bands, you will still need to select a multiple subjects or single subject program to start. At the elementary level, teachers provide instruction for all subject matter and many choose to major in education, liberal studies, child development, psychology, or the instructional language. The middle and high school levels require more in-depth knowledge in a specific area. If you plan to teach at the secondary level—middle and high school— it would be wise to major in the academic field and the instructional

---

[8] The National Center for Education Statistics website on teacher salaries: nces.ed.gov/programs/digest/d20/tables/dt20_211.60.asp?current.asp

[9] Kelly, S., & Northrop, L. (2015). Early career outcomes for the 'best and the brightest' selectivity, satisfaction, and attrition in the beginning teacher longitudinal survey. *American Educational Research Journal, 52,* 624–656.10.3102/0002831215587352

language you are passionate about if you are not a native speaker of the language. Do not worry or feel that you are stuck if you have already chosen a major or program. It is easy to change majors, and once you have earned one teacher certification, you will have the ability to take competency exams to demonstrate your level of proficiency in a different content area to earn another credential. For reference, I earned my undergraduate degrees in Psychology & Social Behavior and French at University of California, Irvine. I joined the Multiple Subjects Credential Program at California State University, Fullerton, used my undergraduate degree in French to demonstrate mastery of language to obtain a Single Subject: French credential, and took two methods courses that helped prepare me for Single Subject: Foundational Level - Mathematics and Single Subject: Foundational Level Science exams.

Student-Teaching Placement. If you have the choice to be placed in a program specifically for dual immersion, definitely select that option! I promise that you will have a more authentic experience and learn tips and tricks firsthand from your mentor as you practice in immersion classrooms. If there is not a program specific to dual immersion at your university of choice when you start your certification program, I highly recommend mentioning that you are interested in dual immersion. Thus, when time comes for student-teaching, your program coordinator could place you in a dual immersion class with your instructional language, if there are opportunities. Please note that high school world language classrooms are not the same as an immersion classroom unless the program is designed as the continuation of the elementary and middle school immersion programs. We will address this difference later.

During your undergraduate and/or credentialing program, there may be some state level tests that you will be required to pass. Depending on your selection of the elementary (multiple subjects) or the secondary (single subject) credential, the number of state competency exams you need to take will vary. The program in which you are enrolled will help you identify and prepare for specific exams you need to take. Depending on your state, you may also need a language authorization attached to your preliminary credential to demonstrate your language and cultural competency. Ask your university program for clarification regarding these requirements and their associated costs. Oftentimes, when there is a teacher shortage in a specific content area, there are programs that will pay for or reimburse candidates for the exam costs upon receipt of a passing score.[10] Once you have passed the necessary exams and successfully completed the program, your university will connect your information with the state commission so that your preliminary credential will become valid and you may be able to start looking for employment options. Your school district or parish where you are hired may also help with updating your state profile with your credential and authorization as well.

Scenario 2: Alternative Pathway Teachers
Hoorah! You had other professional plans in mind but realized that you would like to be a dual immersion teacher. Thank you so much for joining this teaching force that needs your linguistic talent and cultural passion. Even though you already have a bachelor's degree but not in education, or you have an equivalent degree in education from another country, you will still need to obtain a teaching credential from your state. I am making the assumption that you have already volunteered in dual immersion classrooms hence you want to teach in it. If you have not yet done so, I highly recommend that you do. Shadowing a teacher, working with the students, and seeing the planning and organization that goes into teaching a language immersion program will help confirm your decision.

Do your research. It is important that you check with your state commission's regulations and options for alternative pathways. Furthermore, depending on the state, there may be up to four exams

---

[10] Thank you, California Lottery, for supporting public education. To learn more: www.calottery.com/who-benefits

that you will need to pass. Unfortunately, there are no means around these exams at this time. Most alternative programs have flexibility with the understanding of necessary monthly financial support. Programs such as New York's NYC Teaching Fellows[11] and NYC Teaching Collaborative[12] have an "expedited summer immersion training experience" or a "residency experience for an entire school semester," respectively. Other programs, such as CalStateTeach[13] in California allow you to work as a district intern at a school while you are enrolled as a credential candidate in a state program. Instead of an intense, one-year credential program, these programs are three to four years because you are teaching full-time simultaneously. Some school districts and parishes, such as Los Angeles Unified School District[14], have their own internship programs where you can apply directly.

Be patient and proactive. The application process and the notification of your acceptance into these alternative programs generally take about one year. Thus, if you have an inkling that you would like a change in career, start doing your research to find the proper path and develop a paper or digital trail. One of my colleagues learned recently that despite regularly volunteering in classrooms for two school years, working as a classroom assistant, and being a long-term substitute teacher in a dual immersion program, she will still need to complete over 160 intern hours to be enrolled in the alternative program because the paperwork is not retroactive. Had she reviewed the paperwork process when she started her exploration to teach in a dual immersion program, these precious hours could have been counted toward her progress.

The hurdles will feel like they are impossible as you transition from one career to another at times, most times. Be consistent. Find a growing dual immersion school with a working culture that you

---

[11] Information on NYC Teaching Fellow: nycteachingfellows.org
[12] Information on NYC Teaching Collaborative: nycteachingcollaborative.org
[13] Information on CalStateTeach: www.calstateteach.net
[14] Information on LAUSD's iCAPP: achieve.lausd.net/districtinternprogram

embrace and if possible, get connected with human resources and their dual-language program coordinator at the administrative level. They will be able to point you in the right direction or let you know the programs they have available so that you can get started. There is a high demand for bilingual, biliterate, and passionate teachers. When they see your drive, they will know your worth. You may not necessarily be placed at the exact school where you started volunteering, however, the administrators will definitely think of you when opportunities arise.

✧ ✧ ✧ ✧ ✧ ✧ ✧ ✧ ✧

You are not alone in this process, whether you select a traditional or alternative path to earn your teaching credential and language authorization. There are multiple systems of support for you, especially when you are on an alternative path. When you have a moment, take a look at the national bilingual job boards that are available on the websites for NABE[15] and ACTFL.[16] You are needed and you are necessary in our growing profession.

We are finally at a time and place where "bilingual" is a celebrated word and language proficiency in more than one language is seen as an asset. Be proud of the language and culture that you can share with your students. Help the heritage speakers recognize the power and representation of their native language. Create a space where monolingual children have the opportunity to discover a new language and its cultures around the world. You are a bilingual, bilterate, and bicultural role model who our future leaders need to see in our anglocentric environment even though English is not the official language of the United States.

---

[15] Website to NABE's Career Center: careers.nabe.org
[16] Website to ACTFL's Career Center: jobcentral.actfl.org/jobs

You are amazing and you rock for wanting to share your linguistic and cultural knowledge. I believe in you. You've got this!

Your Cheerleader,

Valerie

LETTER 2 CHECKLIST

Everyone:
- ☐ Write down your reasons for wanting to be a teacher. It will be a foundation that will ground and re-inspire you when you feel frustrated, beaten, and lost. I still refer to mine at least once a year.
- ☐ Check if your state participates in the Seal of Biliteracy.[17]
- ☐ Determine your teacher certification path: Traditional or Alternative.
- ☐ Visit Teacher Certification Degrees[18] as a starting place for your certification process research. You can also start your research with "[state] teacher credential programs," look for the official state website and find their list of accredited or approved programs.
- ☐ Visit associations such as the National Association for Bilingual Education (NABE) or the American Council on the Teaching of Foreign Languages (ACTFL) to learn more about the support you can have as a dual immersion teacher.
- ☐ Optional: Research the average teacher salary in your state, school district, or parish where you wish to teach.

Traditional Pathway Teachers:
- ☐ Determine if your state has an undergraduate education degree that includes a teaching credential or a separate credentialing program after you have earned your bachelor's degree.
  - o If it is a separate program, determine your major.
- ☐ Research universities that have state-approved undergraduate or certification programs that will support your pathway.
- ☐ If you are not a native or native-like speaker yet, look into courses at your university of choice for majors, minors, and

---

[17] Seal of Biliteracy: sealofbiliteracy.org
[18] Teacher Certification Degrees: www.teachercertificationdegrees.com

opportunities to study abroad to gain better linguistic and cultural competency.

Alternative Pathway Teachers:
- ☐ Research the multiple pathways to obtain your teacher credential with the keywords "[state] alternative pathways to teacher credential"
- ☐ Gather your college transcripts. If you have a transcript from another country, look for companies that will translate and evaluate the transcript.
- ☐ Search for teaching opportunities in the national associations' career center job boards and write down options that interest you. There may be opportunities within driving distance or you can plant the possibility of moving to a different city or state.
- ☐ Determine your strategy and write it down. Speak to the human resources department at the school district or parish of your choice that has a dual immersion program to know their suggestions and proposed pathways.
- ☐ List family members, friends, and colleagues who support your decision to become a teacher. The hurdles can be huge. Having a supportive network helps a lot in this transition.

LETTER 3: ROCKING YOUR INTERVIEW AND SAMPLE LESSON

Dear Future Dual Immersion Teacher,

I am so excited that you are moving forward with your language passion to teach in a dual immersion program. This is probably one of the best adventures you will go on professionally. First, let's secure that job. Contrary to popular belief, just because you speak the instructional language does not mean you qualify to teach in a dual immersion program, even though there is a great need for bilingual teachers. Some schools conduct a first-round interview and if it goes well, they ask you to teach a sample lesson on a different day. Other schools have both the interview and the sample lesson on the same day. When you have passed the application screening and they invite you to the interview, be sure to listen carefully (despite the adrenaline and excitement) so you know the school's expectation.

The interview. In most situations, the principal and a panel of teachers, specialists, and a parent of the community, will be present for the interview. For an in-person interview, it is best to arrive at least five minutes in advance, let the school secretary or front desk clerk know of your appointment, and patiently wait in the lobby until a school staff accompanies you to the interview space. In an online interview, log in to the meeting two to three minutes in advance to be in the virtual waiting room while the panel prepares for the interview. As you are waiting, make sure your name appears correctly, fix your hair and camera angle,[19] and test your microphone and speaker by using the settings icon. If your backdrop is slightly unkempt, opt to use a virtual background that is representative of you. To go the extra mile, you can use the logo or mascot of the school.

---

[19] The top of your face should be above the middle line of your screen. Optimally your face, neck, and shoulders occupy two-thirds of the screen.

When you arrive in the interview room, each panel member will probably already be seated and have reviewed your submitted cover letter, résumé, and letters of recommendation. The principal will speak first to introduce him or herself and the rest of the panel will do the same. Fight the nerves, smile, try your best to not fidget, and say hello to each person after their brief introduction. Sometimes, the principal or other administrators do not speak the instructional language. So, a team teacher or parent will be the language representative. They may ask you to speak to them in the instructional language to verify your language competency, accent, and fluency. Do not feel shy or awkward that you will be speaking in a language that not everyone understands. You know the language, so use it to the best of your advantage. Note: It is ok to translanguage when you use popular educational terms and jargon.

Depending on the number of people present at the interview, each panelist will most likely ask you at least one question. Due to the time limit of an interview, you may have only two minutes to answer each question. Some of the questions they ask will seem trite and obvious while others may be more difficult to answer. Either way, it will be good to have succinct and practiced answers that can be supported if/when follow-up questions are asked. Listed below are interview questions that I have been asked or have asked interviewees. They are not exhaustive and do not appear in any particular order. I hope they help you prepare for your interview.

Interview Questions
- Tell us about your language pathway and teaching experience.
- Why do you want to be a dual immersion teacher?
- Why do you want to be a teacher at this school or district?
- Do you have a preferred grade level that you would like to teach? Why?
- How do you differentiate a lesson for students who have different language levels?

- Aside from teaching in the classroom, what other interests can you bring to our school community?
- How do you feel about parent participation or involvement in your classroom?
- Describe a time when you encountered a parent who was unhappy with something in your class. What did you do to resolve the issue?
- What is your classroom management style?
- What is your policy on student behavior?
- What happens when a student continuously disrupts your lesson?
- How well do you work in a team? What do you do when you disagree with a team teacher?
- What kind of support do you think you will need as a dual immersion teacher?
- For elementary teachers: What subject are you most excited to teach? In what subject do you feel you will need content support in the target language?
- How do you celebrate your students?
- Explain how you build and keep a positive classroom environment.
- What is your proficiency level and experience in using classroom educational technology?
- What is your experience in creating curriculum or curriculum development?
- What would a person who knows you well say you still need to improve?
- Here is some data. If this data set is representative of your students next year, what would be your first step?

- What do you know about PBIS[20]/MTSS[21]/RTI[22] and how do you implement these frameworks or processes in your classroom?
- How will you challenge the heritage speaker or scaffold for non-native speakers in your classroom?
- How will you ensure that other countries and people who speak the target language will be represented in your instruction, instead of the mainstream, dominant population?

Please do not fret. Not all of these questions will be asked in your interview. However, these are questions that you should consider as a future dual immersion teacher. Many situations will arise that involve these questions and you will need to have a response to them. Hopefully, the credential or teacher preparation program or your experiences as an assistant, substitute teacher, student teacher, or district intern will have helped you in developing some of these responses.

If time permits, you should ask questions, too, especially if there are things that are still unclear. In no particular order, here is some important information that you will need to know as an incoming dual immersion teacher at the school:

- Which immersion model does the school follow: 90/10 or 50/50?
- If it is a 50/50 model, which subjects will you be teaching in the instructional language?
- What grade level will you be teaching?
- Is there a set of curricula in the instructional language that has already been purchased?
- What type of support is there for a new immersion teacher?

---

[20] PBIS stands for Positive Behavioral Interventions and Supports. More information: www.pbis.org

[21] MTSS stands for Multi-Tiered System of Support. More information: www.cde.ca.gov/ci/cr/ri/mtsscomprti2.asp

[22] RTI stands for Response to Intervention. More information: www.rtinetwork.org/learn/what/whatisrti

- Are there specific training or strategies that should be implemented in the classroom (e.g. Project G.L.A.D - Guided Language Acquisition and Design, Kagan's Cooperative Learning, Comprehensible Input, Thinking Maps, etc.)? Will you receive training on these methods?
- Is there a budget for you to attend conferences to learn and connect with other immersion educators in your language?
- What technology is available for teachers and students?

The answers to some of these questions should be discoverable on the school's website, such as the model of immersion program used and the instructional strategies they have in place. It would be important for you to do your research about the school before the interview. If there is not a set of adopted curricula, do not worry, as Letters 10, 11, and 12 will guide you through the process with important points of consideration. Nevertheless, it is an important question to ask because you may need to start planning and organizing when you are offered a position. I hope that you will have a successful interview which will lead to an invitation to teach a sample lesson.

The sample lesson. Most immersion schools require a sample lesson so they can observe your interactions with students, verify your language competency, and evaluate your lesson planning ability. Here are steps to rock your administrators' and panelists' world during your visit: Dress the part and be confident, present a detailed lesson plan and identify the specific standard you will teach, use only the instructional language with the students, have the necessary materials for the lesson, use pictures and images to help the learners build vocabulary and independently produce it in the activity, and lastly, place culture at the center of the lesson. Yes, that sounds like a lot and all of the components may not be required by the establishment, but it will help you stand out from the rest of your peers who are also interviewing for the position. Here is each part in more detail.

Dress the Part and Be Confident

For the day of your sample lesson, wear clothing that is professional yet comfortable in which you can easily teach. If you do not generally wear a dress and heels or stiffly ironed dress shirts, this would not be an ideal day to wear them for your sample lesson. If you will be teaching a sample lesson to an actual class of students, make sure you have clothes on that will facilitate your movements with the specific age group. Bending over with a low-cut top, kneeling in a skirt, or continuously pushing up the sleeves to your dress shirt while working with students may be uncomfortable and a distraction to you, the students, and the administrators. Remember: You know the language, you prepared the lesson plan, and you are going to rock the lesson. Your confidence will shine through when you are not worried about tripping and falling, your dressing riding up, your pants not secured, etc. Keep in mind that the dual immersion program wants you as much as you want to be there. It's true!

Write a Detailed Lesson Plan

Having a prepared and detailed lesson plan for your interview panel will be the difference between a good and great sample lesson that will set you apart from the other interviewees. It may be a laborious task, especially when you write the instructions you will provide in both English and your instructional language, however it will help you teach a thoughtful, prepared lesson while helping the observers understand your actions and student expectations, especially if they are not speakers of the instructional language. Use a template that you are most accustomed to for the lesson plan or go with the simplest form and provide the following information: Title of the Lesson, Number of minutes for the lesson, Standards (depending on your state's adoption, world language standards, and perhaps, ACTFL World Readiness Standards), Lesson Objective, Materials, Steps (Hook, Body with independent practice, Closing), and Measures of Growth. Be sure you have chosen one (and only one) academic content standard that you want to achieve (e.g. CCSS ELA RL.2.1 Ask and answer such questions as who and where to demonstrate understanding of key details in a text[23]). Sometimes a lesson can address multiple standards, however, this will most likely be a seven to ten-minute mini-lesson (unless they tell you otherwise), so focus on only one. Your state's world language standards and ACTFL Standards will focus more on the language production and cultural competency aspects. Remember, as a dual immersion teacher, you are teaching academic content *and* language simultaneously. Make sure that the activity the learners complete is measurable and reflective of the standard(s) you choose. There are times when the administrators observing your sample lesson do not speak or understand your instructional language, however they will be able to follow along seamlessly because of your lesson plan. The more specific you can be in your lesson plan written in English with key words, sentences, and student expected responses or sentence frames in the instructional language, the more appreciative the non-target language speaking panelists will be, especially when it comes to possible dialogue you may have with your students. No worries, there will always be a person who does speak the instructional language, even if the person is a (future) parent of the program. Make sure you know the grade level of your audience so that the lesson is appropriate for their age and language proficiency. Unless the school gives you a specific subject to teach, choose a subject and topic that you know well. Let your creativity and individuality shine. This is my absolute favorite part about teaching. You can find a sample lesson and a lesson template on www.empowered-consulting.com/immersion

Use Only the Instructional Language
This should be obvious; however, I am addressing it because this has been an issue in my observations. While preparing for a sample lesson, one of my mentees asked with a worried look, "but how will they understand me?" Instead of teaching the sample lesson to a class, she would be teaching the interview panel. My response was to use photos, images, actions, realia, facial expressions, and body

---

[23] The full standard has all the components of who, what, when, where, why and how.

language necessary to lend herself to be understood. The key thing that sets dual immersion instruction apart from bilingual or world languages classrooms is the fact that we only use the instructional language with repetition and circumlocute with academic words when necessary to ensure that our students can understand. We create an environment in which our students are literally immersed in the instructional language. Remember, you are going to be in a situation where your students will consistently not fully understand you. So, you must use all the means necessary to be understood. You can simplify the language, have them repeat multiple times while using total physical response (TPR), write the words and provide a drawing to depict meaning, and/or model the expectation. Your observers want to see your interactions with learners who do not understand your language. They want to see your pedagogical skills and the way you scaffold the language for your learners. If you can impress them and help them learn something new in your instructional language with the activity, then chances are, you will be hired for the position.

Bring Your Own Materials
Once you know to whom you will teach the sample lesson, make sure you bring all the necessary materials to make the lesson a great one. If you need copies made for an entire class, I am sure the school can do that for you. Nevertheless, this means that you should arrive 20 minutes in advance of your sample lesson appointment so there is time for the office staff to help you make the copies. If you have specific pictures or images that need to be printed, that should be done on your own time and dime. Think of these printed products as an investment for your future class and for the great lesson you would have created already. Stay organized and set out everything you need in your teaching space before you start your lesson. The last thing you want is to be fumbling and searching for materials mid-lesson.

Lead with Culture
As a dual immersion teacher, a main part of our profession is to share the language's culture with our students. This means that the texts,

images, and resources that you use should be a reflection of the language and culture. The best and easiest way to do this is to use authentic resources. The term "authentic resources" is defined as items that were created in the native language for native speakers. When you lead with culture in your lesson, student curiosity and interest will naturally develop. It could be something as simple as learning about farm animals and the various onomatopoeia that we use for their sounds. For example: A duck says "quack" in English, "coin-coin" in French, "cuac cuac" in Spanish, and "gua-gua" in Mandarin.

✧ ✧ ✧ ✧ ✧ ✧ ✧ ✧ ✧

So, that is it. It is a long list of things to do to assure that a 20 to 30-minute interview and a 10-minute sample lesson will be successful. Nevertheless, you will be so happy that you did them! I have coached several teachers for competitive positions for which they were worried they would not be selected, but they were the chosen one for the school. Some of them have said that their administrators were blown away by their level of thoughtfulness and preparedness for the sample lesson following the steps that I had provided. Be confident. Follow these steps. You've got this!

Your Cheerleader,

Valerie

LETTER 3 CHECKLIST

- ☐ Prepare your answers to the sample interview questions.
- ☐ Research the school and district to find information pertinent to your position.
- ☐ Select a lesson in your instructional language that you have taught as a student teacher, experienced as a teacher's assistant, or know well as a substitute teacher. Write it out and prepare the materials. This can be your go-to lesson for your interviews.
- ☐ Prepare an interview and sample lesson outfit that is professional and comfortable. It is ok if it is the same outfit each time.
- ☐ Observe sample dual-immersion lessons that are available on the Teaching Channel,[24] Center for Applied Linguistics (CAL),[25] and Center for Teaching for Biliteracy,[26] among other resources to see best practices that teachers are using and replicate them in your own lessons.

---

[24] Teaching Channel: www.teachingchannel.com
[25] Center for Applied Linguistics: www.cal.org
[26] Center for Teaching for Biliteracy: www.teachingforbiliteracy.com/sample-pd

LETTER 4: GETTING READY FOR THE FIRST DAY OF SCHOOL

Dear Dual Immersion Teacher,

Congratulations! You had a rockstar interview and sample lesson and you were offered a position in a dual immersion program. Woohoo!! I am absolutely doing the happy dance with you. Now comes the planning and decorating. I am sure you have a ton of thoughts and ideas for classroom decorations. Maybe you have an entire Pinterest board created with themes already. Go you! Maybe you need to walk around your local dollar store or the dollar section at Target for inspiration, that works too. Whatever the case may be, know that you will be spending money. This is the unfortunate and often unspoken part of teaching. Teachers spend a lot of our own money in our classrooms. We do it for ourselves and for our students. Your classroom is going to become your second home, so why not make it a space in which you know you and your students will enjoy? Do not fret, you do start accumulating things throughout the years and trading items with your colleagues is always an option. I only spend a bunch when I am changing my classroom theme or changing grade levels. I often reuse the items I have, too! My teacher credit union offers a $1000 loan at no interest the month before school because they understand that this could be a big spending month for educators. You can check with yours, so that you do not garner extra debt at this time. Yes, we do have to be smart about our expenses!

As an elementary teacher, if you are hired before the school year ends, ask your administrator if you could see your future classroom. This will help you know the dimensions and the amount of wall space available to decorate. Then ask if the school has days for you to go in before school starts so that you can start decorating and setting up. If you are hired during the summer, this is also an important question to ask. The summer days, usually one to two weeks before the first day of school, were the moments when I had been able to make friends with new colleagues and catch up with ones I already knew. If you are brand new to teaching, you may be lucky and be able to borrow supplies from some nice neighbors, too. Not to mention, you may ask for expert advice on how to attach things to certain parts of the wall and learn about the mandatory items that will absolutely need to be posted.

If you are a middle or high school teacher, things may be a little different. From my experience as a world language teacher, cute, themed decorations are not as important. However, there were anchor charts, images of countries that spoke the instructional language, a map, a poster of common phrases, and a set of classroom expectations that I did staple to my walls. Just like the elementary classroom, there were mandatory items that needed to be posted as well.

Depending on the grade you teach, the items you place on your walls will be different. For my classes, I always had a word wall for reference, a math and language arts wall to display student work, and a wall for art projects. Here are some tricks I learned throughout the year for displaying student work:

- **Student work walls.** I used 12" x 12" scrapbooking sheets; the theme of the scrapbook sheets was whatever was on sale at the store that I liked. I am on a budget! Each student had one sheet and it was stapled to the wall. On top of this sheet, I placed a clothespin hot glued to a thumbtack aligned to the top center of the paper. This way, I could easily clip on and take off assignments, as opposed to stapling each assignment on the wall. It was an ultimate time saver when I consistently switched assignments for display.
- **Hanging work.** For hanging other schoolwork around the classroom, I used a clear plastic lacing cord that had a large paper clip tied to each end. On one end of the cord, the paperclip was pulled open like the letter "L" and I was able to put that between the ceiling board and the metal borders. The other side was still a paperclip so that I could clip on and

pull down student work easily. The length of the cord was determined by the height for me to reach up both of my arms to touch the bottom of the paper clip. You will have to adjust the length of the lanyard according to the average standing height of your students to make sure the hanging works do not hit their heads.

- **The word wall.** My word wall was prepared by cutting 22" x 28" poster boards in half lengthwise to have 11" x 28" sheets. Each sheet was laminated so that I may write with a whiteboard marker and erase the words at the end of the year, if necessary. Each of these "long" strips were for a letter or a complex sound. At the kindergarten level, my words were put up once a week, one board at a time. At the secondary level, the entire alphabet was posted and I added words with pictures as we progressed throughout the year. I referred to this wall every time we were writing so my students learned to use it as a reference.

- **Labeling student supplies and materials.** At the elementary level, class rosters were in constant flux and were usually not stable until the first six weeks of school. So, I would save labeling student supplies until the very last minute when the class roster was "finalized." I printed student names with the classroom roster number on the 1" x $2\frac{5}{8}$" labels that have 30 stickers on each sheet. For kindergarten, I had one sheet that included every student's name and class number. For other grade levels, it was part of the first day activity to go through our inventory. My students were given one sheet of 30 labels and wrote their names on the labels to stick to all their supplies: workbooks, journals, pencil boxes, water bottles, communication folders, etc.

- **Class roster numbers.** Using classroom student numbers helped me stay organized. I always included their roster number (#1-36) in front of their name. It made it easy to put things in order and immediately find the student who was missing something.

- **Shared supplies.** You will need to decide which supplies will be shared commodity in a table group and which ones will be individual student responsibility as supplied by the teacher. With COVID-19, sharing supplies will be difficult without proper cleaning. It may be a good idea to make sure that each student has their own pencil box filled with supplies. On the first day of school, my students always had in their teacher-provided pencil boxes: 2 sharpened pencils, an eraser, and a box of crayons (thick ones for kindergarteners and regular ones for second grade and above). Later in the week, after a proper introduction and modeling of usage, a pair of scissors with student numbers written on there for easy identification and a glue stick were added. I also had a drawer of lost and broken crayons that students could claim and use if they did not have a particular color.
- **Pencil sharpening.** I disliked the disruption of a pencil sharpener in the middle of a lesson, so each student was equipped with two sharpened pencils in their pencil boxes. Nevertheless, I also had a bucket to place pencils that needed to be sharpened and another bucket for already-sharpened pencils. My students learned that they could make a pencil exchange quickly when it was writing time. At the beginning of the school year, I would sharpen pencils in the "needs sharpening" bucket at the end of each day. As the school year progressed, that task was transferred as a student's job to do during the school day.

✿ ✿ ✿ ✿ ✿ ✿ ✿ ✿ ✿

Sneak Peek. To ease tension and anxiety in preparation for the first day of school, my school hosted a Kindergarten Sneak Peek. This one-hour event was generally only for transitional kindergarten or kindergarten students who have never been a student at the school. I am in favor of this event and found it to clarify parent-child and student-student relationships. It generally took place a few days or one day before the first day of school. My kindergarten classroom was usually not fully ready, but it was presentable. At the event, I would have four centers set up: Coloring, LEGOs or building blocks, beads for making bracelets or necklaces, and puzzles. Each student also had one task that they needed to accomplish: find their name on the board written on a large apple-shaped paper, take that apple, and place it on their selected seat for the first day of school. As their first teacher at the school, I did not know the students or their histories, so it was easier for me to let them choose their seats. This activity was in three-folds: 1) I observed to see if the child was able to recognize his/her name and I took note of the amount of assistance their parents provided; 2) They selected their seats for the first day of school which saved me from placing students randomly on my seating chart; and 3) The students knew the location of their seat for the first day of school which reassured the parents that their child would not be lost in the classroom. I allowed the students to change their seats if they saw a friend come in and the seat beside them had not already been occupied. Almost all students attended the Kindergarten Sneak Peek, but if they did not, it was ok.

At Sneak Peek, I greeted each student with a high-five and "bonjour." Some students were comfortable and reached their hands out for a hug, so I gave them a hug. I wore a sign that said I could only speak in French for the parents. The students and their families walked around, visited, and played in the classroom for about 45-60 minutes. During this time, I walked around and made mental notes of extroverts, introverts, native speakers, ability to share and clean up, preferences for playing alone or together, and other traits that I found interesting. I listened to parents who had questions and concerns. I spent probably 10-30 seconds with each student. I also collected parent data at the time they signed in: their email addresses and if they had access to the Internet at home. If Google Forms had been available in 2012, this would have been streamlined and I would not have had to spend an hour decoding parent scribbles on paper after the Sneak Peek. With those e-mail addresses, I sent them a thank you note for attending Kindergarten Sneak Peek which included the link to our class website and my wish list of glue sticks, tissues, and baby wipes, if they were feeling generous.

If your school organizes a Sneak Peek, embrace it and use this time to your full advantage. If your school does not have this type of event before the school year, talk to your principal about the possibility to host one the next school year. All the reasons for having one are provided in the upcoming third book of this series, *Navigating Dual Immersion: An Administrator's Companion Before and Beyond the School Year.*

All this said, there are some educators who strongly oppose teachers working in the classroom before they are required to be back on the school site. I understand their perspective as this is voluntary, unpaid work time. As teachers, we give a lot of our time and are not compensated for it. Some educators who have decades of experience feel that it is the system taking advantage of teachers, especially elementary teachers. I agree. Nevertheless, I also know that for my own sanity and organizational purposes, having only one day in my classroom prior to welcoming students is not something that I am able to accomplish. Here is some reassurance: The first day of school preparations do become easier and faster with experience. By my last year in the dual immersion classroom, I had created enough reusable items and had constructed solid relationships with student families that I was able to enlist help from previous students' parents who had siblings joining my class. Usually, three days prior to the first day of school was sufficient for me to feel prepared for the big day.

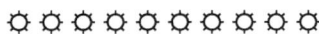

✿ ✿ ✿ ✿ ✿ ✿ ✿ ✿ ✿

Designated curriculum. Whether you are the first teacher of a new dual immersion program or an experienced teacher joining an established program for the first time as an immersion teacher, creating or adapting to a new curriculum is a daunting task. Due to the relative novelty of dual immersion programs, there is a limited selection of "boxed" curricula that is ready for use. A lot of supplemental material will be necessary and unfortunately, some items may come out of your own pocket depending on the urgency of these items. I spent a lot of money my very first year buying read aloud and picture books for my classroom over the summer before school started. I was glad I did because the materials I requested through the school needed approval at the district level and I received them in March/April when the school year was close to ending.

There are pedagogical practices that you can use in a dual immersion program that are akin to an American education, such as the calendar routine and shared read aloud at the early elementary level. For the first six weeks of school, it is all about survival (at the lower grades), setting classroom norms, and reviewing previously learned concepts for the other grade levels. Do not worry if you do not have a curriculum or are unfamiliar with the new materials you were provided. The important part is knowing your routine, creating a warm learning environment that gets students excited about being in class with you, and speaking the instructional language 100% of the time as a language model for your students.[27]

✿ ✿ ✿ ✿ ✿ ✿ ✿ ✿ ✿

There are a lot of things to think about as you plan for the school year, and it is easy to feel stressed. Not to mention, COVID-19 has changed a lot of teaching and learning, including our classroom practices and the preparation necessary. Your sneak peek event will probably look different as well, since students will not be sharing toys and you will not be able to high five or hug your students. You can use this opportunity to model non-touch ways to greet your students: air high fives, a bow, foot taps, etc. You can find a set of slides that shares non-touch greetings on www.empowered-consulting.com/immersion.

---

[27] There are some educators who translanguage in the upper grade classrooms to demonstrate to students the flexibility of their language repertoire and to give value to both languages.

Do not let all the tasks overwhelm you. There are things that you can control and others that you cannot. Take a few deep breaths. Know that your students will be excited to be at school, to learn from you, and to play with their friends. Nothing needs to be perfect, and your classroom can grow with your students. The most important part is that you follow the district and the school's safety guidelines. You can work on the vision and routine that you want to provide for your students and then break it down to achievable tasks. Your students are lucky to have a passionate, dedicated teacher like you.

To help calm your nerves in preparation for the first day of school, you can use the checklist that follows this letter. Work together with your grade level team to see the things they have done to prepare for the first day of school. Remember: You do not need to reinvent the wheel.

If your first day of school is a Monday, I hope you have a restful weekend. Take time to relax and rejuvenate because you are about to jump on a great adventure that does not provide very much rest for the next six weeks. You are going to be a rockstar teacher. I believe in you. Be safe. You've got this!

Your Cheerleader,

Valerie

LETTER 4 CHECKLIST

☐ Ask your administrator to see your future classroom.

☐ Inquire about when you would be able to start putting your classroom together.

☐ Inquire about school-wide rules and safety policies. Translate them into your instructional language, ONLY if it has not already been done.

☐ Ask your administrator if there is a set of curriculum or instructional materials that you and your students will be using.

☐ Ask your administrator or school secretary if there is a classroom budget to purchase materials. If they have already purchased supplies for you, ask for the supply list, so you know the items you will still need to supplement.

☐ Here is my usual list:

    ☐ 4x the class set for pencils, Ticonderoga Beginners for kindergarten

    ☐ 1x the class set pink erasers

    ☐ 1x the class set + 5 extras of pencil boxes, pencil pouches, recipient for supplies

    ☐ 1x the class set of scissors* (first year only)

    ☐ 3x the class set for crayon boxes. My students receive a new box every trimester.

    ☐ 2x the class set for markers

    ☐ 2x the class set for colored pencils

    ☐ 1x the class set + 5 extras of flexible rulers*

    ☐ 1x the 100 sheets of 30 labels (this can last for 1 or 2 school years)

    ☐ 12" x 18" construction paper in all shades and colors. 2 packs per color. White, black, light and dark brown, gray, pink, magenta, red, light and dark blue, light and dark green, light and dark purple, yellow, orange, salmon, beige, etc.) Refill as necessary.

    ☐ 20 sheets of 22" x 28" white poster board (first year only)

- ☐ 4x the class set for glue sticks (parent donations will come in handy)
- ☐ 4x the class set of 12" x 12" scrapbook sheets, theme pending, reusable
- ☐ 1 roll of clear lanyard
- ☐ 1x class set of birthday crowns
- ☐ 2 boxes of giant paper clips (first year only)
- ☐ 4x the class set for wooden clothespins (first year only)
- ☐ 4x the class set + extras for thumbtacks (first year only)
- ☐ 1 glue gun* (first year only)
- ☐ 1 pack or more of glue gun refills

☐ If you do not have a theme for your class yet, go to your local dollar store and see which themes are available for decorations and supplies. Let that be your inspiration.

☐ Ask your grade level partner(s) about their classroom rules. If they have a digital version, ask if you can replicate or modify it.

☐ If your school is going to have a sneak peek (of any level), create a Google Form or a Microsoft Forms (depending on your district's technology adoption) that you can make available on portable devices at the entrance of your classroom so that parents can sign in. QR codes are a great option! You will only need the following information:

- ☐ Student First Name
- ☐ Student Last Name
- ☐ Student Nickname, if applicable
- ☐ Father or Legal Guardian 1 Full Name
- ☐ Father or Legal Guardian 1 Preferred email address
- ☐ Mother or Legal Guardian 2 Full Name
- ☐ Mother or Legal Guardian 2 Preferred email address

☐ With a permanent marker, label the items with an asterisk above with TeacherLastName # (ie. Sun 24). These items may last for several school years and will only need replacement as they break or go missing.

- ☐ Pencil boxes and student materials can be labeled with the sticker labels when the roster is final.
- ☐ If you have a student roster, use the label template and create your student list for labels.
- ☐ Use the labels and create a "This belongs to Teacher Name" and stick it on everything you have purchased for the class, especially books and reference manuals. You will be glad you did this.

LETTER 5: THE FIRST DAY OF SCHOOL

Dear Dual Immersion Teacher,

Hoorah to you because today is the first day of school. I know you are a mixture of exhaustion and excitement because you have been working away making sure that your classroom is as perfect as it can be to greet your students. There is really only one thing you need to know about the first day of school: You will SURVIVE. The kiddos are just as nervous and excited as you are. You are going to spend the next academic year together and they will be exposed to a brand-new language or continue to deepen their language knowledge through your guidance and facilitation. Your goal for the day is to just get through it in the most efficient, friendly, and fun way possible, while staying in the instructional language and establishing classroom norms. Here are some fun activities to try with your students that are multifold:

- Start the day with a letter to them. Whether you want this as a part of your morning meeting on the first day of school or at a different time, it is up to you. But share your letter with them. Let them know about your nerves and your excitement, your favorite subject, what you are most looking forward to in the year, if you have pets, are married, have children, etc. Anything that you think they would like to know about you and the year they are going to have with you. You will need a lot of pictures and actions to make your letter comprehensible especially for the students who are just starting the language. Then, if they can, let them write a letter to you about them regarding their first day of school. What do they hope to accomplish this year? What should you know about them that you will not necessarily find out? If they are not able to write letters due to age, then let them record a message to you (via Flipgrid, Seesaw, or any other platform) or draw a picture that is representative of them. Their response to you does NOT need to be in the target language if they do not know it. For students who have been in the program, sentence frames will be great! With my middle school students, we watched the video "I wish my teacher knew…" and I let them share their stories with me. I was able to use those letters to get to know the students better throughout the year.

- To build a classroom community, let students interview each other in a guided conversation. There is an EduProtocol,[28] called Frayer-a-Friend created by Jon Corippo and Marlena Hebern. The interviewer provides four descriptions of the interviewee and asks if they are OK with the descriptions provided. Then they find out four things that the interviewee likes, four things that they dislike, and my favorite, the interviewee's dream pet - real or imaginary. Then they switch roles. While they are interviewing each other, you walk around and ask several students if they can share one of their descriptions, likes, dislikes, or dream pets. This provides time for them to mentally prepare to share with a group. They can also say no, too. When everyone is done, you have specific volunteers! When you ask the person to share something they like and they do, ask the rest of the class who also likes and enjoys the said item. Be sure to ask why to develop further understanding. Then ask if there are students who do not like that item and ask why. Go gaga over how cool the dream pet - imaginary or real - would be. This helps the students know that you are excited to get to know them *and* they get to know each other on another level as well.

- Give a tour of the class. Ask your students to form two lines and walk around the classroom, from wall to wall. Let them know where the classroom supplies are located, what to do in the classroom library, when to use the pencil sharpener, which spaces are off limits, etc. Then ask them what they would like to add to the classroom. What more do they need

---

[28] Hebern, M., & Corippo, J. (2018). The EduProtocol field guide: 16 student-centered lesson frames for infinite learning possibilities. Dave Burgess Consulting, Incorporated.

to help them learn? They can draw it, write it, or share it out loud. It does not matter. But this gives the students the opportunity to let you know that you are there for them and that the classroom belongs to them as well.

- Depending on the grade level, share a read-aloud with them. You would be surprised by how much the upper elementary, middle school, and high school students still enjoy read alouds. Once again, depending on the grade level and time allowance, you can have a follow-up activity with the reading. Drawing their favorite part, citing their favorite line, making a connection to the story, or if they did not enjoy the story at all, what book would they rather you have read?

- ENJOY your recess, prep period, and lunch. This is your break time. Laugh, cry, and/or catch up with your colleagues.

As much as you feel like there should be some academic learning going on during the first day of school, rest assured that your students are doing some serious social learning. As we talk more about the importance of social and emotional learning (SEL) in our technology-filled world, the first day of school is a social time where students learn about each other, about you, and about the classroom routine. If you teach at the elementary level, maybe you will spend the entire day with them or maybe there is a class switch in the middle of the day. Either way, they will get to know that routine. If you teach middle or high school, your students will be *tired* of the review of the syllabi and rules that they are getting from every single teacher. Let your class be a break from that. You can go over the syllabus tomorrow or at the end of the week. Better yet, you can gamify your syllabus by transforming the information into EduProtocol: The Fast and the Curious. Unless you have very specific rules that are different from the norm, most students know the behavior and academic expectations. Use this first day of school to get to know your students and let them know of the routine.

With my elementary students, I always ended my day with a class meeting. We talk about the things we accomplished during the day based on our posted schedule and one thing that made them smile - a new friend, finding their old friends, etc. - and I give them a heads up on the activities and schedule for the following day. I usually end with a game, so that we could conclude the class on a positive note. My kiddos loved this end of the day routine. Some of the games we played were: Down by the Banks, Duck, Duck, Goose, and What's My Name. Feel free to incorporate your own games and ask your students for suggestions when you and they are ready to share the space.

My middle and high school students ended the period on their first day of school with an exit ticket - their letter to me about the things they wish I knew about them, an information sheet with their birthday, favorite candy, etc. so that we could celebrate their birthdays in class.

You are going to feel *exhausted* at the end of the school day, especially this first day. Your nerves are in overload because you have probably made over 1,500 decisions on this day alone. Embrace the fatigue. Give yourself time to breathe. You are going to have an amazing year with your kiddos. I believe in you. You've got this!

Your Cheerleader,

Valerie

LETTER 5 CHECKLIST

☐ Write out your schedule for the first day with specific time blocks and activities. This will serve as a guide. It is ok if you do not actually follow the time blocks.

☐ Determine your classroom routine. Do not worry, it will not be set in stone.

☐ Write a letter to your students.

☐ Gather pictures of you that support your letter to help make the letter more comprehensible.

☐ Decide if you want to start with technology on the first day of school if you are in a 1:1 device classroom.

☐ Pack a snack and lunch, even if it is leftovers or takeout.

☐ Select a "Back to School" read aloud in your instructional language and have a few others as backup for the next few days.

☐ Plan a whole class game that can be easily played by everyone.

☐ Secondary level: Determine your exit ticket.

☐ Optional: Look over EduProtocol: Frayer-a-Friend and EduProtocol: The Fast and the Curious as they can be easily adapted for your classroom.

LETTER 6: THE FIRST WEEK OF SCHOOL

Dear Dual Immersion Teacher,

You are a rockstar cultural ambassador. In a time of globalization and a decrease in the number of college students and adults learning a language, you are making a difference in the K-12 pipeline. You are helping develop bilingual/biliterate citizens at a young age, supporting the pride of the home language of heritage speakers, while opening doors for more cultural understanding. Thank you!

You will feel stressed and fatigued when the students go home. Anyone who has told you otherwise is in denial of their true feelings. Rejoice in the silent and peaceful moments during recess, lunch time, and dismissal. Give yourself time to breathe. Do some deep breathing exercises (breathe in for 5 counts then breathe out for 5 counts. Repeat 5 times or more depending on your needs) to calm your nerves and to be present with yourself. Please do not give in to the overwhelming feeling or give up. The work you are doing with your students is incredible and it takes time to get the hang of it all; even seasoned teachers get the first week of school fatigue.

Just like the first day of school, the first week is about survival with a focus on setting classroom routines. Create a list of the non-negotiable processes that you would like your students to follow every day. Remember that you are building classroom culture and student social and emotional learning this week; academics can wait. Having a seamless routine is a top priority because a positive and organized classroom culture, with students knowing the processes, will be extra helpful when they are learning academic content. Go slow to go fast. Let me say that again: Go slow to go fast. The heavy lifting of content is a lot easier to provide and for students to digest when they know the expectations. So, the important item right now is to establish your routine.

Here are some routine things to consider:

- Lining up in the morning - How do you want your students to line up? Single file, arrival order, number order, etc. What will be your quiet signal and the signal to walk to the classroom? Is there a line leader?
- Entering the classroom - Where do students put their backpack, snack, water bottle, and lunch bag? Do they sit on the carpet or at their desks? Do they need to take out specific materials (homework folder, library book, etc.)?
- Morning message and/or bell work - What do the students do once they are inside and waiting for others to get settled?
- Water and restroom break - What is your policy on water and restroom use? Does your school require a hall pass? Do students have to raise their hand to ask for permission? Do they use sign language to communicate their needs? For TK and Kindergarten, will you go together as a class during specific times at the beginning of the year if there is not a restroom attached to your class?
- Pencil sharpening - Do you have a pencil exchange system? When can they use the pencil sharpener?
- Checking out materials - Is there a checkout system if they need to borrow markers, crayons, rulers, etc.? Where can they look for these things?
- Shared group materials - Are your students sitting in groups, and do they have shared materials (book bucket, rulers, scissors, glue, markers, crayons, etc.)? What is the process for using these materials? What sharing strategies will you use and ask of your students?
- Classroom library - This is different from the school library. When are they allowed to go to the classroom library? What is the process to get a book, so that your organized and leveled library does not get messy? Can they check out books to bring home? How often do they get to check out books?
- Returning class work - Is there a particular spot to return their work? Do they go by an assigned number or look for their

name in their "mailboxes" or return to the corresponding tray with their class? Is there a system in which they should write their name?

- Snack - Are snacks eaten indoors? Outside during recess? Can they share? Where do they put their trash? What happens if there is a spill? How will they ask for help to open a snack?
- Lining up for recess or dismissal - Will you dismiss them by rows or table groups? Individuals? Do they line up in alphabetical order?
- Computer, iPad, Chromebook - If you have a class set or have a cart, how will you hold your students accountable for its use? What is the process of unplugging and recharging the materials? How will you protect these materials? What will happen when one is not working?
- Classroom jobs - Will you have jobs for your students? It is often nice to give students the opportunity to feel a part of the class through job assignments. Depending on their age, you can either assign rotating jobs or let them apply for jobs every quarter. Here are some common jobs: Line leader, door monitor, librarian, snack/lunch monitor, messenger, telephone monitor, or materials distributor. There are multiple ways to get students involved in the classroom. Jobs can be rotated weekly, monthly, or any time system that best suits your class!

✿ ✿ ✿ ✿ ✿ ✿ ✿ ✿ ✿

As you build your class culture this week while establishing the classroom routine, you want to discover information about your students as they learn about each other and about you. It would also be important to see the language skills that your students have retained over the summer. So, some reading, writing, and math review would be helpful. This is not hardcore academic content. These are warmups and an informal diagnostic to see your students' current language competence. Here are some activities that you can do:

- If you had taught this grade or class previously and had students write letters of advice to the new group of students, let your current students read those letters and talk with each other about their findings. Open this up to a class discussion about their questions, concerns, and events that will occur this school year. This activity helps you recognize students' ability to read, comprehend, and speak in the target language.

- Let students write to their future selves. What do they hope to accomplish this school year? What are some things they would like to learn? With what subject do they think they will have a hard time? For the lower grades, let them draw a picture of their current self and another of what they think they will look like at the end of the year. You can use string to measure their height and trace their hands and feet for comparison. Put everything in an envelope with their name. It could be a self-addressed envelope if you would like to send these letters to them at the end of the school year. Or, you can share these with them again at the end of the school year. This will help you identify students' fine motor skills and writing abilities, including writing conventions, and if they know their home addresses.

- Find a 3-Act-Math activity that is age appropriate for your students. For the younger grades, I love Graham Fletchy's Cookie Monster[29] to review counting. For the older grades, How Much Dew[30] is fantastic to see your students' understanding of fractions. These are fun, estimation and reasoning-based answers that allow for students to make errors. It is beautiful for creating confidence in math while using language.

- Host a math talk. This activity helps with building classroom routines by taking turns talking and respecting other classmates' ideas. Simultaneously, it helps you see your students' mathematical understanding and reasoning. The bonus is that there are no incorrect answers! Show students a

---

[29] The Cookie Monster 3-Act-Math by Graham Fletchy: gfletchy.com/the-cookie-monster/
[30] How Much Dew 3-Act-Math by Graham Fletchy: gfletchy.com/how-much-dew/

series of four images and ask them which image does not belong. The silver lining of COVID-19 is that many teachers have created these materials and have shared them. All you need to do is a quick Google search.

- Discover the awesomeness of EduProtocols Smart Start.[31] Marlena Herbern, Jon Corippo, and Kim Voge have worked together to make the beginning of the school year easy with embedded lesson frames that will help carry your school year. EduProtocols is a teacher's life and time saver. Many of the lesson frames are also available in multiple languages already. You will need to replace the Smart Start content materials with items from your instructional language so that you stay true to the dual immersion model.

✿ ✿ ✿ ✿ ✿ ✿ ✿ ✿ ✿

Not only is this first week a time to build a positive classroom culture, but this is also a crucial week to build positive relationships with your students' parents. Just as you are nervous, they are also worried about their children and their adjustment to a new class and teacher. This is especially true for parents whose first child is in a dual immersion program and participating in a language they do not speak at home. Parents who are sending their second, third, or older child to school know the drill a little better, so they are not as anxious. Nevertheless, they still need to know that you see and care for their child. Some parents will want to reach out but will hold themselves back because they know you are busy. I know that you are busy, too. But, reaching out to them via a phone call first during the first week will help them see the incredible teacher you are. The call does not have to be long. I have gotten my message down to 30 seconds with each phone call. A personalized email does not have the same effect. Make the phone call. To help you prepare for your phone call, this is my message:

---

[31] EduProtocols Smart Start: www.eduprotocols.com/smartstart

Hi Mr. or Mrs. Roger, this is Mademoiselle Sun! I am Chloe's kindergarten teacher this year. I wanted to make a quick phone call to welcome you to the class and let you know that Chloe volunteered in class today to introduce herself *in French* to her classmates! I think she's making some friends in class. Please know that you can always email me when you have questions. You can also find out more information about this class by visiting our website. I hope you have a wonderful day and I look forward to seeing Chloe tomorrow!

Yes, I called every student's parent or guardian. If I could not reach mom, I called dad. Yes, I was guilty of calling mom more often than I called dad. I am trying to be better about gender responsibilities. If they answered, I said my practiced and student adapted message, with appropriate pauses for them to respond. Sometimes my phone call would go to the answering machine, and I would leave my message. I made this phone call for multiple reasons:

1) I started the year with a positive phone call for every child to create a positive relationship with the parents. For the rambunctious child, this may be the only positive message or phone call the parents would hear all year.

2) The parents understood and saw in action that I had their student's best interest at heart and truly embraced an open door for communication with this first call.

3) I had the opportunity to hear firsthand from the parents the information their child had shared with them about the first week of school.

4) For the parents with whom I left a voice message, I usually received a response. They would write me an e-mail, or a few would call back to chat. They were always grateful to have received the message.

Because I shared with the parents that I would be calling all the families during the first week, the majority of them were respectful of my time. I also set a 3-minute timer for each call. When it reached the 3-minute mark, I would gently and politely remind the parent that I was trying to reach all the parents and that general information about the class and about me could be found on the class website and during Back-to-School Night. With that, I was usually able to end the call and make the next one. I divided my list of 26 students into 4 sets, so I called 6-7 families every day. With many of the calls lasting 30 seconds to 1 minute, I was usually done with the set list in under 10 minutes. These 10 minutes each day were extremely meaningful as it set up the rest of the school year with an inclusive, positive tone.

For my middle school students, I called the parents during my prep periods. I was lucky to have had two prep periods throughout the day, so I made sure to call 15 families during each prep. The middle school parents were generally shocked to get my phone call. They wondered if their child had done something bad. They would be pleasantly surprised to hear that I was merely reaching out to welcome them to my class and to help them get involved since their children did not share very much with them. This was also the time that I got the parents in Google Classroom as guardians so that they would receive notifications after they had accepted the invitation. With new student information systems syncing with Google Classroom, I am not sure if this step will still be necessary.

Here are the steps to build your phone message:
1. Start with a greeting
    a. Example: Hello Mr. or Mrs. [Parent last name], this is [Your name] and I am [child's name]'s [grade level] teacher this year.
2. Welcome them to the class
    a. Example: I wanted to make a quick phone call to welcome you to our class and let you know that [Student + positive action observed] in class today.
    b. Note: If the student said something in your instructional language, mention it. It is important for the parents to know that their child is using the

instructional language, especially for families who do not speak the language at home.

3. Let them know the means to know more about you and the class

   a. Example: Please know that you can always email me (provide your email address) when you have questions. You can also find out more information about this class by visiting our website (a shortened and accessible URL).

4. Close the message with a positive message

   a. Example: I hope you have a wonderful day and I look forward to seeing [student] tomorrow!

✿ ✿ ✿ ✿ ✿ ✿ ✿ ✿ ✿

There are definitely a lot of housekeeping items to keep track of during the first week. Remember, it is all about survival for this week. If there are two main things that you are able to accomplish during the first week of school, getting enough sleep and making the phone calls home should be your two priorities. Sleeping well will help you stay calm and patient during major decision-making moments throughout the day. Making the positive phone calls home will save you a lot of time and misunderstanding in the future. I promise. This is the one thing that I wish I knew during my very first year of teaching. You want to build a strong relationship with the parents and be on the same team when issues arise regarding student learning and achievement. You will be tired, yes, but you will rock this first week of school. I believe in you. You've got this!

Your Cheerleader,

Valerie

LETTER 6 CHECKLIST

- ☐ Learn your students' names.
- ☐ Solidify your classroom routine.
- ☐ Create your phone call message.
- ☐ Divide your class list into achievable chunks and set aside 15 minutes each day to call the parents.
- ☐ Create a check list of all the forms and information you need to collect from your students.
- ☐ Find class community building activities.
- ☐ Go to bed at a decent hour to get the rest you need.

LETTER 7: BACK-TO-SCHOOL NIGHT

Dear Dual Immersion Teacher,

WOOHOO! You have made it through your first week of school. You are alive, you are amazing, and you have started building bridges with your students and their parents or guardians. Everything may seem like a giant whirlwind with multiple highs and lows each day. If it were not for your teacher plan book, you probably would not know the amazing things you have achieved, or remember the day's date. Perhaps you feel today is Friday, because you are completely exhausted. I feel you.

There is a big event around the corner, Back-to-School Night, and there is a lot of buzz. Some teachers do not like this evening, others embrace it. I, personally, loved BTSN for its data sharing and gathering value. It is 15 to 45 minutes of time that I could communicate with the parents about the incredible things their children will accomplish. Furthermore, I am able to speak to them in English without worrying that their children would hear me.

The game plan. If you have a grade level team and you plan with them, work together to have the same presentation so that you demonstrate a united front. It is almost certain that one of your colleagues already has a presentation slide deck ready to go from the previous year, and you could use that after a few necessary modifications. There is no need to reinvent the wheel. Once the core deck is ready with your team, make a copy, rename the file with the academic year, and personalize it to fit your class.

In the case you do not have a grade level team to borrow information, a sample can be found on www.empowered-consulting.com/immersion. Here are some key information items you need to have in your presentation:
- Your name, email, and school phone number + extension

- Your parent room representatives, if you have that at your school
- Some information about you, ie. the number of years you have taught, your interests, your experience with the instructional language, or any random information you would like to share
- The immersion program and percentage of time you will use the instructional language and the name of your English partner, if there is one. This should be brief.
- The overall daily schedule
  - Include library, media/STEM lab, gardening, or other regular extracurricular times that are embedded in the school day
- Your classroom behavior expectations and communication and the school wide behavior policy
- Your homework and classwork expectations and return policy
- Assessments, progress reports, and report cards information
- Optional: Access to your class website
- Optional: Technology integration for parent logins and family connections

I mentioned above that I used this time to collect information from parents. When they arrive in my classroom, they sit at their child's desk which has not changed since Kindergarten Sneak Peek. On the desk, they get a paper form that asks:

- Communication and language preferences
- Their ability to speak the instructional language
- The preferred parent to reach when a phone call is needed
- Their access to the Internet
- The desire to help decorate the classroom afterschool
- The desire to volunteer as a language speaker in small group instruction
- The desire to volunteer for non-student interaction tasks
- The desire to volunteer during holiday activities

- The desire to share a cultural lesson with the students in English or in the target language
- If they had received the classroom weekly newsletter
- If they had already accessed the class website
- If they are technology savvy and would like to help me with tasks from time to time
- Anything else that I needed to know about their child

I also had a sheet circulating in the classroom where parents signed up for a weekend to take home André, our class mascot. Some parents chose the first few weeks of school, while others chose specific weekends or a date that was close to their child's birthday. A techy parent volunteer later helped me place the dates of André's visits on the shared Google class calendar.

For BTSN, I speak clearly, but quickly. I only take questions at the very end because I want parents to listen carefully to the information that I am providing them. When I see a hand raised, I would kindly ask them to wait until I finished the entire presentation. Most times, their questions were answered by the end of the slide deck. BTSN is a time to relieve parents of their anxiety and help them know the expectations of your class. Oftentimes, they want the reassurance that their child will learn the instructional language and be successful academically. I give them those reassurances, and I also remind them that these students are kids who need time to explore and play. I let them know that my job is to ensure their child loves learning and coming to school. If they happen to learn some language along the way, that is awesome!

You will occasionally have a parent who is inquisitive about dual immersion and would like to ask all types of questions about assessments, language acquisition, speech delay, and all that jazz. You do not have to answer these questions if you are not comfortable. You can direct them to your administrators to help you with these questions. There are also resources posted on the EmpowerED Consulting website that you can link on your class website to help the parents learn more about the ongoing research in dual immersion and second language acquisition.

I hope you enjoy your Back-to-School Night where you have the ability to match a student with their parents. I hope you close the classroom door at the end of the evening with a big smile, feeling good and ready for the year ahead with all the information you have gathered, including the help that you can have from the parents. This is going to be a great year. I believe in you. You've got this!

Your Cheerleader,

Valerie

LETTER 7 CHECKLIST

- ☐ BTSN slide deck – prepare it with your grade level team for uniformity, if possible.
- ☐ Create a parent survey to collect information. This can be a Google or Microsoft Form or be paper-based.
- ☐ Create a family sign-up sheet for your class mascot's home visit, if you have one.
- ☐ Enjoy your time connecting with parents at BTSN and do not look at the completed surveys until the following work day. Give yourself a break.

LETTER 8: THE NEXT 6 WEEKS OF SCHOOL

Dear Dual Immersion Teacher,

Boom! You have made it through the first few weeks of school. I hope you made some great connections with the parents of your class through the individual phone calls. They are key stakeholders, and it is important that you build positive relationships with them. This will also give you more credibility when you call them about a behavior or character issue.

During these next six weeks of school, you will continue to build the classroom routine that you had determined during the first week of school and will start reviewing the previous year's content. A routine should be a process that the students become familiar with and can become their own responsibility without your guidance. Whether it is the morning meeting with the calendar routine, the classroom library checkout process, or coming into the classroom or dismissal, these routines should become well-oiled and autonomous. The minute or so that you have available during the autonomous morning routine will give you time to take attendance before the school secretary calls you with a gentle reminder.

If there is a routine that does not sit well with you as a teacher or does not work with your class, change it. You are the captain of this ship, and you move along with the currents; it does not help to go against the tide. Nevertheless, give each routine at least two full weeks of practice before you decide that it does not work well because it does take time for students to learn new habits. Also, ask yourself the purpose of the routine - what is the objective of the routine? If your students are able to give you feedback about the routine, ask them what would make the experience better. This helps your students know that they are part of the classroom community, and their voices are important. This also helps you learn about your students' needs, and it gives you the possibility for clarification if there is something that does not click right with the group.

One of the most important routines is small groups. This is where instruction is differentiated for your native speakers and non-native speakers. Start with simple and independent tasks that are age appropriate for your students. The idea is to help them get used to working independently in three groups without disrupting the small group that you have working with you. Make a list and divide your students into the number of stations you are going to have by their language or academic proficiency levels. I do not suggest having more than six students in one group. For kindergarten and first grade rotation practice, I set out cars, coloring pages, puzzles, beads, and books in each center. I let my student know that we are practicing so we will be spending only five minutes at each station. I explain their task at each center on the carpet before dismissing them to their respective centers. When I see that everyone is at their center and ready to begin, I set the timer. During the five minutes, I make sure the students are silent or using whisper voices and following the task. When the timer rings, the students have 30 seconds to clean up, and they line up in a specific spot beside their rotation table. Once everyone is in line, I know they are ready to rotate. And boom, they rotate in 30 seconds or less. I see everyone is ready to work, set the timer, and the cycle begins again. The goal is to help them get used to moving, completing work independently, using a non-disruptive whisper voice, cleaning up when the timer rings, lining up, and getting ready to move again. Once they have a solid grasp on the rotation system, slowly add in activities that they have completed with you and can complete independently. Each rotation task should take approximately the same amount of time.

If you are at a school that has strong parent involvement, small groups instructional time is a great way to invite instructional language speaking parents into your classroom. I was fortunate to have a set of parents who were available to join my class during small groups twice a week. They completed sound recognition games and writing activities with my students while I worked on specific math or language arts materials for my differentiated groups. They got a peek of the classroom, and my students had the opportunity to hear French from native or native-like speakers. It was marvelous and a win-win situation! I should note that I only invited parents into the classroom after my students were used to the rotation system.

COVID-19 makes small group rotations a little bit more difficult since students should not be sharing materials or moving around the classroom unnecessarily. Your small groups can be students who are sitting near each other at the table groups. It can also be adapted to be independent work time for most of the class while you work with three to four students at a kidney table.

No matter how you structure differentiated instruction, know that it is necessary in your schedule to meet the learning needs of your dual immersion students. Native and native-like speakers in your classroom will need to be challenged while the non-native students will require scaffolds and support to learn the academic content and language that you provide.

✿ ✿ ✿ ✿ ✿ ✿ ✿ ✿ ✿

I was at a school that was equipped to allow me to integrate technology into my class using iPads, so a routine I had in my class was appsmashing with ChatterPix and Book Creator. During the first week of class, while learning the routine of iPads, —finding a partner, getting an iPad, not removing the protection balls, and waiting for instruction— my students also learned to use ChatterPix. It is an app that will make any picture "talk" for 30 seconds with a voice recording. It is an app that provides room for creativity and personalization for the student. After learning to introduce themselves, their task was to find a partner and create a talking picture introducing themselves with the sentence frame: Bonjour, je m'appelle _. J'ai _ ans. (Hello, my name is _. I am _ years old.) They worked in pairs so that they could help each other take a picture, record, and decorate the talking image. Every child's work was compiled into an eBook in Book Creator. The file was stored in my Google Drive and linked in an e-mailed newsletter to the parents at the end of the week. Note: ChatterPix allows you to draw a "mouth" anywhere on the picture. While most students are respectful of the location of the mouth they draw, it would be a good idea to let your students know where you would like the mouth to be drawn. Some kiddos can get quite creative, especially when we introduce animals, if you know what I mean!

The silver lining of COVID-19 is that every teacher and school-age student had the opportunity to experience technology integrated into their learning. There are many amazing tools available for you to use to deliver your lessons and create independent guided work for your students of all levels. The goal with technology integration is the ability to let students become creators of their work to demonstrate their learning, rather than complete an assignment where everyone has the same, exact responses. There are moments, such as letter and number formation, where the work will look the same. However, the application and conceptual understanding of a letter or a number can be demonstrated to you differently. It is your job as a teacher to make sure that you are helping your students learn in the most optimal way. The Universal Design for Learning (UDL) Framework[32] will guide and help you create opportunities where your students will be able to demonstrate their learning in multiple facets.

The important idea to keep in mind when integrating educational technology in your lessons is to recognize the learning curve of the tool and being consistent in its use. A general rule in technology integration is to never teach academic content at the same time as introducing a new tool. The cognitive load would be too high for your students who are juggling a language, academic content, and a tool. Depending on the age level of your students, sometimes logging in to a chromebook is a process that will need to be taught, much less

---

[32] Universal Design for Learning (UDL): www.cast.org

accessing an application or program within the chromebook. Despite the continued narrative that our students are digital natives, there are processes that are school specific and our students need to acquire them in order to use their devices seamlessly due to the extra protections set in place by the school district or parish. If you realize that there are some students who are more technology savvy than others, recognize their special talent and let them be your peer helpers. It is a symbiotic relationship: You appreciate their extra hands and support while they enjoy the special privilege of being your assistants.

✿ ✿ ✿ ✿ ✿ ✿ ✿ ✿ ✿

We are in the 21st century and I highly recommend that you have a class website if you have not established one already. If you created one during COVID-19, I hope that you found it to be a useful space for your students and their parents and guardians. Remember, the website is only as useful as your regular updates and frequent references to it as a resource for classroom information. Most school districts use Google Apps for Education and the New Google Sites makes it simple to create a website with a few clicks. If you are unsure about steps to creating a website, there are many tutorials on YouTube created by educators that will walk you through the process. Furthermore, I suggest that you create a tinyurl or bit.ly with your class' name so that visitors can easily remember and access your site without typing in the long address. I recommend that you keep the same website every year, updating your "About Me" page as necessary, and archiving outdated information to make them no longer visible to visitors. This will save you from reinventing the wheel and re-creating a new, shortened URL each year.

A class website is different from a Google Classroom. Google Classroom is where you post classwork or homework assignments, and parents can be included as a guardian to receive e-mail notifications of the student's work completion. Your class website is a way to communicate with the parents and the local or global community. This is the space where parents can discover more about you and stay updated regarding the events in their child's class. I believe my class website helped my students' parents feel comfortable knowing the academic content the students were learning and stay connected to me as their child's teacher.

I conducted a pilot study[33] in 2015 regarding necessary parental support in dual immersion programs. The study included a survey to better understand the support parents needed, especially when they did not speak the instructional language at home. Many parents mentioned that they felt at a loss in supporting their students academically or in accessing the academic materials that the students were learning. I also discovered that most of their questions and concerns were usually related specifically to academic content or classroom routines. In the same survey, 100% of the parents said they visited my class website at least once a week and over half of them said they referred to it at least twice each week. A select few said they referred to it at least three times each week. Thus, having the website helped resolve a lot of issues and concerns for my students' parents. Note: I created my class website using a personal Google account because I wanted to have full access to the website with or without the school district. Access to my creation would be lost if my school account closed due to employment changes.

Here are the pages that I had on my website:
- Homepage/Welcome page - It included a class photo and welcomed viewers to my class
- Class calendar - This was a shared calendar through Google that included the school master calendar and a class calendar that included each student's birthday, field trips, Thursday Folder volunteers, André's home visit (our class mascot went home every Friday), library days, and other random events that I felt the parents would like to know about our class.

---

[33] Results to the pilot study can be found here: www.empowered-consulting.com/immersion

- Newsletters - This page was updated every week with academic content that I would be teaching. It included:
  - The week's letter name, sound, and specific vocabulary words
  - The sentence frame focus
  - The read aloud book of our unit theme and a video of it being read, if available via YouTube
  - The math number focus and concepts
  - The song of the week and its video via YouTube
  - And any other information I felt pertinent for them to know - Spirit Week, special events, volunteers needed, etc.
- Teacher's Corner - This page contained a brief autobiography so the parents would know who I am. It was also linked to my full teaching résumé (without my address) so that they could have a better understanding of my educational background, work experience, and the multiple "badges of honor" I have earned. This seems like a lot of information to share, however, I would rather they have access to detailed information I openly provided than information they randomly discovered during a Google search to learn more about me.
- Wish list - This page was necessary because I had supplies that needed to be regularly replenished. Baby wipes, boxes of tissue, and glue sticks were at the top of the list.
- Resources - This page had links to educational websites that I found helpful for students to practice French at home and research articles that addressed language learning, speech delays, and student performance in dual language immersion.
- eBooks - All of our class-created eBooks were linked on this page. This page was password protected so that only parents of that school year had access.

Almost all parents have smart phones now and should be able to access your website and newsletter. However, it will still be important to survey all the families regarding access to technology. Depending on your area and parent accessibility, you may need to have both digital and printed copies of your weekly newsletter.

✿ ✿ ✿ ✿ ✿ ✿ ✿ ✿ ✿

I hope that your routines are starting to flow and that each day during these six weeks are getting easier for you. I also hope that you are enjoying the classroom culture that you have started to build with your students and that you are making necessary adjustments so that they all feel heard and welcomed. Teaching is all about the connections you make with your students. For some of these kiddos, you are their one consistent adult. As much as your instruction is student-centered, it is also important that you feel comfortable in your space.

Teaching dual immersion is not an easy profession and I am glad that you are on this journey with your students. Keep it up. You are planting seeds that you will see blossom in multiple ways. I believe in you. You've got this!

Your Cheerleader,

Valerie

LETTER 8 CHECKLIST

☐ Reflect on your classroom routines and make necessary changes.

☐ Create a class website. It does not have to be perfect. You can build it as the year progresses.

☐ Learn an instructional technology tool and integrate it in your lessons consistently.

☐ Challenge yourself and your students by introducing a new tool or a new way to use a tool each month.

☐ Recognize a few technology savvy students and embrace their support the next time you use technology in class.

LETTER 9: GETTING PARENTS INVOLVED AND ONBOARD

Dear Dual Immersion Teacher,

Your students' parents are your best allies. They also have a stronger voice than you for changes to happen at the school site and at the district level.[34] It is necessary that you build a strong, positive relationship with the parents in your classroom. After the initial phone call during the first week of school and once routines are established, it would be a good time to invite parents to participate in various activities in your classroom. I understand that not everyone has the same comfort level with a parent in the room, so it is all good if this is not your jam. I have an open-door policy, but I also do not let any parent come into my classroom without a specific purpose. I always have a reason for their presence. Once they have completed their task, I usually let them know it is time for them to leave so that they do not linger. It will be up to you to figure out your comfort level. Here are ways in which parents have helped me in my classroom.

Small Groups in Early Elementary
Depending on the neighborhood, oftentimes, my language colleagues and I were the only language models. So, I tapped into the parents' language capacity during small group instruction. I gave them tasks like leading a game where students practiced letter names and numbers, helping students scribe for their drawing, or signing on/off students using various technologies. I had small groups twice a week, during a specific time frame, so I asked parents who were available to sign up. This only worked well for parents who had regular flexibility in their schedules.

---

[34] Parents having a stronger voice for change is both a fortunate and unfortunate thing. This is more reason to ensure that you are allies.

Weekly Folders

If your school is like my school, we had stacks of information that went home on Thursdays in a convenient Thursday Folder. All of the school and district communication flyers go through that folder. If you have eager parents who do not speak the instructional language but would like to contribute to your classroom, you can have a rotating schedule for this duty. It sounds silly, but you will need to train the parent volunteer to gather the information and stuff the folders in the way you need them done. You also need to train them to leave once their task is complete. I liked consistency and did not like having to train different parents each time there was a change, so I had one parent who helped me throughout the entire school year. She did not speak French, but she was involved and saved me a lot of time. Both of her children loved having her in the classroom, even though she did not interact with the students. Once she was done with the folders, she left the classroom.

Cultural Experiences & Holidays

I hope that as an immersion teacher, you are open to other cultures and practices as well. During specific holidays, various parents would come and share their cultures with my class. I would ask that they explain to me the materials they would like to share a week in advance and we would come up with an activity to do together. Generally, they had 30-45 minutes and spoke in English, unless they were comfortable speaking and sharing in French. I had a student's father who was a musician and a drummer. He brought his instruments and accompanied all of our music shows that year. My students loved having their parents in class and the experiences gave them a sense of pride because of the offering their parents were able to provide. Parents who spoke other languages were also invited to read or complete activities with our students as it was validation of the importance and value of other home languages. Check with your parents if they have a special talent or idea that you would like for them to share with your class. I am certain they would love being present in their child's learning experience.

Classroom Decorations

Aside from decorating my classroom at the beginning of the school year, I left the artistic freedom to create my class themes to the students' parents each month, starting in late September and in time for Halloween. I would send an e-mail to see who was available on a specific day and usually two to three parents would reply. I had supplies, but they were invited to bring some too. They would come to my classroom after school and I would show them the supplies I had and the materials they could use to staple, stick, or pin. I trusted their artistic taste and skills and left them in my classroom while I planned with my grade level team, language team, or attended a staff meeting. When I came back, my room would be transformed. It was a major time saver! Oftentimes, the kids would be in the classroom helping as well so they had a special peek. The following month, the same parents or another set of parents would come and take down the previous month's material and put on decorations for the new month. Apart from the first year where I specifically bought items for each month's theme, I recycled all of my decorations the following years. With parents bringing in a few new items, there was always something to be used. It was awesome!

✧ ✧ ✧ ✧ ✧ ✧ ✧ ✧ ✧ ✧

While having active parent participation is an absolute delight for me, this is your classroom, and you are in control of the space. You do not have to allow every parent to volunteer, nor do you have to agree to every parent's suggestion if it does not suit your comfort level. I had a parent who suggested that I do a super elaborate art project with the kindergarteners. We talked for 30 minutes, and I was excited but apprehensive because the project was going to be time-consuming. I was also having a hard time finding ways to tie the project to some academic standards aside from student creativity and fine motor skills development. Well, everything halted when I realized she wanted me to do the project alone. She was not available to help, contribute materials, or gather other parents to help me in this giant endeavor. I gently declined her suggestion and offered to save it for another time.

Parent participation in your classroom, whether it is during instructional time or afterschool is vital to the positive relationships you can build with them. Having this positive relationship makes the hard conversations a little bit easier because they see you on a human level. They know that you are not out for their kid, plotting ways to make their child's school life miserable. They see that their child behaves differently in class. They also see how difficult and time-consuming everything is in the classroom, especially the chaos that can happen with the blink of an eye. They are so much more sympathetic and compassionate to frustrations you may feel after having volunteered. Having them involved in these ways helps you to be on the same team when issues arise.

If you teach in an area that does not have very much parental support due to socioeconomic status, that is ok. Find other means to reach them. Build these relationships. You need them just like they need you. I believe in you. You've got this!

Your Cheerleader,

Valerie

LETTER 9 CHECKLIST

- ☐ Reflect on your comfort level with parent involvement in your classroom then set your boundaries for parent participation.
- ☐ Create a list of tasks that parents can do with quick training from your end.
- ☐ Create a list of parents who are available as classroom volunteers.
- ☐ Categorize parent volunteers with their instructional language ability and match them with the weekly tasks.
- ☐ Ask for parents who would like to share cultural experiences with your class.
- ☐ Decide if you want monthly themes in your classroom and assistance for decoration.
- ☐ Start building relationships!

LETTER 10: ASSESSMENTS

Dear Dual Immersion Teacher,

Assessments. Formative, summative, district-required, state-mandated, tests, tests, tests. AHHHHHHHHH! I am going to say it now to get it out of the way: I do not like the pressure these assessments place on our students nor on us as teachers. Our educational system has become obsessed with data in a way that our students are no longer seen as kids and holistic individuals. They have become numbers, percentages, red or green, proficient, below basic, or the most absurd – far below basic. What happened to the multiple intelligences that we were taught to address in our credential programs when it came to assessments? Well, that is a conversation for a different book. For now, know that official assessments are unavoidable, and we will shift our perspective to recognize that they are indeed necessary for instruction. I will help you discover ways to make it less gut wrenching for your students and for you. For assessments in dual immersion to make sense, you will have to have a good understanding of your grade level standards. Ideally, you also have a well vertically-aligned and articulated language program, but this depends on your administration. Letters to administrators addressing this concept will be available in the third book of this series.

If you are like me when I started, where you are teaching in a brand-new program and there are no assessments in your instructional language, then you will have to create them. Translating the English language arts assessments into your instructional language will be futile. Do not do it. Let me say it again. Do not do it. There are cultural and language differences that will not transfer nor make instructional sense. If you want to be stressed and have kids crying during assessments, then you can choose to translate the ELA assessments. How do you create your own assessments that are meaningful? Know your grade level standards. The standards will be your guide to the competencies that your students will be able to accomplish at the end of the school year. Each standard will almost always need to be broken down into multiple pieces so that it can be scaffolded for the students in terms of their language development.

For example, when I was teaching kindergarten, one of the California State Standard for Reading: Literature was "with prompting and support, retell familiar stories, including key details" (CA CCSS RL.K.2). This would be a daunting task to achieve during the first six weeks of school. My non-native speakers did not even have the vocabulary to speak, much less retell a story! I broke it down with a reading protocol and graphic organizer.

The graphic organizer has three boxes each with the title: In the beginning, In the middle, and In the end. After reading our focus story of the week, which we read multiple times throughout the week, we would talk about the events in the book. I explicitly taught my students one sentence frame at a time. There were not many choices for the events that happened at the beginning of the story. So, after reading the story, I would turn back to the first two pages of the story book. I would ask them what happened at the beginning of the story. We would have a small discussion and build our vocabulary using various sentence frames and vocabulary words. My students and I would draw together in the first box the event at the beginning of the story. Then we would say together, "In the beginning..." The rest of the page would be left empty since we were not working on "in the middle" and "in the end." After a few weeks of practice and I knew my students understood the concept of "in the beginning," I moved on to "in the end." There would not be too much discussion about what happened "in the end" either. So now, we would complete "in the beginning" and "in the end" leaving the middle part empty. Because it was always the same graphic organizer, my students learned the purpose of the document and knew the task to be completed. Within a few weeks, I did not need to explicitly review the task with them as they knew that they needed to draw the beginning and ending of the story we read together. This gave me time to go around the classroom to "scribe" (annotate or write down) student sentences to describe the events directly after distributing the graphic organizer. Then we would bring it back together and my students would share their ideas with everyone. The "in the middle" portion was very open to interpretation since multiple events could be told. In the first teaching of this concept, we would discuss all of the events that happened and I would draw all the events that we discussed on a chart paper. Then, I would model myself thinking about the book and choosing my favorite "in the middle" part that I would draw on my graphic organizer. I would complete the other two parts as well. Before distributing the graphic organizer, I would let my students choose one "in the middle" event that they liked and encourage them to draw that first before working on the other two boxes. There were always a few students who drew two or more events that happened in that portion. Once they were used to using the graphic organizer to demonstrate three parts of a story, retelling a story became an achievable task. My students were able to retell the main events of a story using drawings, language, and sentence frames "In the beginning... in the middle... in the end..." by the end of the school year. Furthermore, because it was a graphic organizer that they had regularly used, they were not stressed when I used the same sheet as an assessment.

For kindergarten, I kept a running list of things that my students needed to know to do: Know the alphabet and count to 100 by 1s and 10s, for example. So, during my morning routine where volunteers came up to do certain activities, I would have my checklist: When a student, Suzi, was leading the alphabet song, could she say all the letter names and sounds? What about when we pointed to random letters? If she could, I would make a mark by her name. One less student to assess. Zoé was leading the count to 100 by ones and by tens. Did she say all the numbers correctly? Did she count by tens to 100? If she did, great! Her name had a mark beside it. These running lists or running records were informal items for me, however, I knew right away the students who could complete certain tasks and the kids who needed extra support to make that happen. It also made me recognize the shy students who did not want to participate in front of the class. This made the individual assessments easier to manage. I knew exactly who I needed to call.

In order to decrease the stress of assessments for your students, formal evaluations should definitely sound like and look like the things that you are doing on a daily basis in your classroom. Know your standards and the objectives of each activity you complete with your students. Time is extremely precious in dual immersion because of the amount of information we need to cover. Not only are we teaching language, but we are also teaching academic content. The amount of language scaffolding that is necessary makes every single one of our activities important in our class.

By the way, not every individual standard needs to be tested! There are standards that you can combine. For example, in the retelling of a story using the graphic organizer, the students' drawing and writing "He is..." or "His name is..." can help me check off the following standards:

- Reading: Literature Standard 2 – With prompting and support, retell familiar stories, including key details.
- Reading: Literature Standard 3 – With prompting and support, identify characters, settings, and major events in a story.
- Writing Standard 3 – Use a combination of drawing, dictating, and writing to narrate a single event of several loosely linked events, tell about the events in the order in which they occurred, and provide a reaction to what happened.
- Reading: Foundational Skills 1 – Demonstrate understanding of the organization and basic features of print, etc.

It is imperative that you spend some time to know your grade level standards, the world languages standards, and the ACTFL World Readiness Standards. You are a language and content teacher.

Without knowing the standards well, you will lose the purpose and objectives of your lessons. Breakdown and scaffold the learning for your students so that they understand and know the tasks you ask of them. Create a running list to help you.

Honestly, as much as I have a hard time with standardized testing, assessments are not so bad if you conduct lessons and activities with purpose and consistently prepare your students with the standards. Learn to know your grade level standards. I believe in you. You've got this!

Your Cheerleader,

Valerie

Ps. It is the district-wide computer assessments in English that I have a hard time digesting. With my instruction in a language other than English, my assessments should be in my instructional language, especially in the lower grades. I have had serious conversations with principals regarding this matter. It is something that will need to be taken to district leadership for more serious consideration in this data collection era.

LETTER 10 CHECKLIST

☐ Have access to and learn your state's grade level standards.

☐ Have access to and learn your state's world language standards.

☐ Have access to ACTFL's World Readiness Standards.

☐ Plan your lessons with assessments in mind.

☐ Use or create graphic organizers that can be reused with other content and as an assessment.

☐ Breakdown a standard into bite-size language development pieces.

LETTER 11: CULTURE AT THE CENTER OF INSTRUCTION

Dear Dual Immersion Teacher,

You are a cultural ambassador. You are a representation of the country of your instructional language. Whether you are a native speaker or a near-native speaker who spent time learning the language, there are multiple cultural aspects that you can bring to your students. All of us who have learned a second language know that it is impossible to learn a language without learning its culture. Thus, how do we regularly include culture in our classrooms without stereotyping groups of people or practices? More importantly, how do we address culture and cultural practices outside of the major holidays of our instructional language?

Even though it looks like you are doing everything your English counterpart is doing, there are multiple layers to your instruction. One of the layers is cultural competence because we are helping shape bicultural students, not solely bilingual and biliterate learners. With instructional choices focused on authentic materials, cultural awareness and practices can very easily be at the center of our instruction. Authentic materials are not just realia. They are materials that were created in the instructional language for people of that language. For example, a bus schedule, a calendar, a newspaper article written expressly for kids, a recipe, etc. Any material where the author's intended audience is the native speaker of that language is considered authentic material. Authentic materials can be a written text, a video, a recorded audio clip, an object, a website, or the like.

It is important to use authentic materials in our repertoire because there are inherent cultural differences in organization or presentation of these items. For example, European calendars start with Monday as opposed to Sunday, and they use military time in their posted information. Their use of images, colors, and print can also be considered. The compare and contrast in the usage of these everyday items provide an insight into the concepts that are considered important to the culture. Another example is a "small eats" menu from Taiwan. This is a rich resource because not only do we learn to recognize food names and popular dishes as part of a food unit, we can also take it a step further for cultural competence and understanding. We can point out the role of "small eats" restaurants in Taiwan and through teacher guidance conclude that these restaurants are mostly a self-service space where efficiency and food quality is the focus rather than the service provided. This comparison is a large contradiction to the attention to service at sit-down restaurants in the United States.

An example for our older students would be an observation of firefighter calendars. I experienced a great cultural surprise while I was living in France. My partner sent me a message to say that firefighters were at his work, and he purchased their promotional calendar. With my American mindset, I said I could not wait to see it and jokingly asked which month he thought would be my favorite. My partner was confused by my excitement and responded with September, my birthday month. I immediately understood his confusion when I saw the calendar. French firefighter calendars contained pictures of these brave men and women in action, literally fighting fires. My partner was shocked to learn about images placed on American and Canadian firefighter calendars. This cultural difference in the perspective of promotional materials could lead to a discussion of means of advertising, consumerism, and any distributed media.

The use of authentic materials at the center of your lessons will automatically bring cultural aspects into the conversation. You will have to choose your resources wisely depending on the performance or proficiency goals of your unit for the materials to tie in seamlessly with your standards. You will have to know your grade level standards in order to bring in culturally relevant and authentic materials. Remember, it will be your job to encourage the questions that bring your students' attention towards gaining cultural awareness and cultural competency. With continuous questioning on your behalf, your students will start to examine their environment with a more critical and intercultural lens. It will be beautiful, I promise. I believe in you. You've got this!

Your Cheerleader,

Valerie

LETTER 11 CHECKLIST

- ☐   Review your units of study for the academic year
- ☐   Find authentic resources[35] that match with your units

---

[35] Leslie Grahn has a collection of authentic materials for multiple languages:
www.grahnforlang.com/authentic-resources.html

Dear Dual Immersion Teacher,

You are amazing. Did I tell you that? You truly are. The reflection and preparation that goes into each of your lessons which follows not only your grade level standards but also world languages standards are noteworthy. I recognize that it takes a lot of time, and I (and your students' parents and administrative team) am forever grateful for the time that you are spending on the instructional materials so that your students have a positive learning experience.

If you are one of the lucky ones, you received some form of curriculum for your grade level from your school and district. I did not have many things and spent a lot of my own savings the first year, but I considered myself lucky anyway. My administrative team believed in me and gave me the creative freedom to plan standards-aligned units and lessons that were fitting for my students. This was a daunting task because I had to create everything. However, I knew my grade-level standards well and I was able to find materials that reflected age-appropriate content, culture, and pedagogy. I cannot say that my instruction was fully student-centered the first year as I had to pilot the airplane while building it, but my creativity was present. To be able to create your own curriculum, you must know your grade level standards. There is no way around it, period.

Several years ago, to my complete surprise, an elementary dual immersion teacher who I mentored told me in all seriousness, "Valerie, the English Language Arts Standards don't concern me because I'm not teaching English." I realized that this teacher was gravely misinformed, and I guided her back to the standards. As an elementary level teacher, your grade level ELA standards are the backbone of your language program. They are your guide in the specific language structures that your students should be learning in your instructional language. There will be adjustments to make depending on your language, but for the most part, consider ELA standards as the language arts standards that your students will need to learn by the end of the school year. Replace the "English" in front of "Language Arts" with your instructional language and make the necessary linguistic adjustments.[36] This is where vertical alignment in your dual immersion program becomes highly important because linguistic adjustments need to be coherent from one grade level to another.

One of the adjustments I had to make for French immersion in kindergarten was the recognition of short and long vowel sounds and blending and segmenting consonant-vowel-consonant (CVC) words. CVC words do not exist in the French language where all three letters are consistently heard. Instead, we worked on individual letter sounds, nasal sounds, and common digraphs. With all the silent letters in French pronunciation, we learned to read with consonant-vowel syllables and then put syllables together. Then, we learned about common irregularities where specific final consonants were generally silent. The administrative team at my school did not speak French, so I had to be the expert on my campus in this case. No, I was not an expert at the French language at the time and I still am not today; the Académie française[37] exists for this specific reason. Nevertheless, I did not make any of my decisions lightly. I consulted the reading programs in France and Canada, spoke with my colleagues at the private French school where I worked previously, did my own research on Google, and discussed my ideas with the other kindergarten dual immersion teachers on campus. You know your instructional language well. Connect with your colleagues and grade level partners of the instructional language across the city or state and do some research on your own so that you understand the justification of certain decisions. Yes, it will be time consuming, but your curriculum will be much more meaningful and reflective of the learning needs of your students and the grade level standards.

---

[36] Middle school and high school teachers continuing the immersion program will focus on the world language standards for your state and think of the language as the content.

[37] Académie française website: www.academie-francaise.fr

You are probably thinking, great Valerie, you just gave a whole lot of work with no specific place to start. Here is where you start if you are starting a brand-new program. If you are in a 50/50 program, look at the adopted ELA materials because most districts like to stay faithful to their adopted ELA program. Moreover, you want to complement the work of your English partner. Here are the steps:

1. Know your grade level standards. What skills in reading, speaking, listening, and writing do your students need to accomplish by the end of the year?
2. Break down the standards and backwards plan. What skills in reading, speaking, listening, and writing do your students need to accomplish by the end of the second trimester? By the end of the first trimester? Be reasonable; some languages are harder to learn than others.
3. Review the adopted ELA curriculum units and their texts. There are generally eight to ten units.
4. Lay out your instructional language materials, read aloud books, and place them into each of the units.
5. Determine a theme that could surround each of your units, if you choose to not use the themes in the adopted ELA curriculum. Using AP and IB themes is a possibility, too!
6. Search for authentic materials that would support your selected themes and areas in which you do not have enough materials.
7. Backwards plan starting with the first trimester (or quarter) goals in mind using the authentic materials you have selected. Here are some sample questions to ask yourself:
   a. How can I scaffold language for my students so that they can reach this goal?
   b. If my students need to write an opinion sentence independently at the end of the first trimester, what opinion sentence frame(s) do I need to teach them?
   c. With the themes I have, where are the opportunities for students to express an opinion?

      d. Will the sentence structure I use be as simple as "I like __. I don't like __." Or more complex "I prefer __ over __ because __." Hint: Your grade level standards will guide you on the complexity of the sentence structure.

  8. Remember, your students are learning language *and* content with you! Be kind with them. It may be that in the first trimester, they understand your request to show their opinion and they are only drawing their ideas and copying the sentence frame "I like [drawing]." At the end of the year, a whole 36-40 weeks later, they are writing independently the sentence "I like [content]."

These eight steps are a very general guide. There are nitty-gritty components that will take a lot of reflection and discussion to ensure horizontal (grade level team) and vertical (language team) alignment in your program. This is a process that takes at least one year. Please do not despair if you do not have a "solid" curriculum.

A 50/50 program offers multiple pathways to support content understanding and language development. It is a necessity that you plan with your English partner to build a solid curriculum; you should never be planning alone if you have a grade level partner with whom you share students. There are important conversations to have with your grade level and language team to ensure that academic benchmarks in language and content are met.

I taught in a 90/10 program, so I did not have to be as attentive to the ELA program in my selection of materials. Nevertheless, I always planned with my grade level team for the 30-minutes of English instruction. You can bet that I incorporated the same listening and speaking skills (and sentence frames) that I was teaching in English into my French instruction.

Curriculum development is a daunting task, and it takes a lot of reflection, discussion, and time. However, once it is complete with cultural components in place, you will be so delighted that you accomplished this great feat. Changing items or switching materials will also be easy because you know the language standards that you were meeting with that resource. Your dedication will pay off in the sense of ease you feel every year here after. To have a more complete guide in the selection and creation of your curriculum, I highly suggest you refer to the Guiding Principles for Dual Language Education, Third Edition,[38] from the Center for Applied Linguistics.[39]

It may take a few years to feel like you have created a good curriculum and that is ok. Mine took four years before I felt it had all the necessary components aligned to the standards at that time. Currently, that same set of curriculum needs additional resources that includes other Francophone countries, minority authors for read alouds, and student representation. Even though curriculum development takes time and may seem daunting, please believe that this task is achievable. I believe in you. You've got this!

Your Cheerleader,

Valerie

---

[38] Guiding Principles for Dual Language Education, Third Edition www.cal.org/resource-center/publications-products/guiding-principles-3

[39] Center for Applied Linguistics: www.cal.org

LETTER 12 CHECKLIST

- ☐ Download the digital copy of Guiding Principles for Dual Language Education, Third Edition, if you do not yet have one.
- ☐ Download your grade level language arts standards if you do not yet have one.
- ☐ Closely review the standards and see where you may need to adjust according to your language.
- ☐ 50/50 Program: Use butcher paper or a digital document and write down the themes of your district's adopted ELA program.
- ☐ 90/10 Program: Decide the themes you would like for your class for each unit.
- ☐ Find time to talk and plan with your grade level team and/or language partners.
- ☐ Ask your administrator to have at least one day dedicated to this planning.
- ☐ Take out the materials you currently have and categorize them into the themes you have.
- ☐ Take note of units where you need more materials.

LETTER 13: TEACHING TEAMS AND PLNS

Dear Dual Immersion Teacher,

Your teaching team is going to be your lifeline in this program. Whether you are the first teacher of the program, or you are a new teacher joining an established program, your team will be your ultimate support. I hope that you have an understanding and supportive team with possible mentors to guide you through your first year in the program. If after a few weeks, you realize that you are at a school site that does not seem to have that, find your PLN (professional learning network) on Twitter, Facebook, an organization such as NABE, ACTFL, or a teacher association that is specific to your language. There are digital chats and discussions that happen on a regular basis where you will find like-minded educators. #Dualimmersion and #duallang are two hashtags to follow on Twitter as a start.

Teaching can be a very lonely profession despite having so many children surrounding you. I have felt alone as the only French teacher at a high school and an electives teacher at a middle school when I first started teaching. No one knows your struggles or experiences in your classroom except for you. However, know this: It does not have to be this way as a mainstream English-only teacher, and it really should not be this way at all for a dual immersion teacher. I strongly agree with a colleague who said along the lines: With our connectivity today, you are choosing to teach alone if you are not reaching out to people on social media when you do not have your own supportive group on campus.

Because I was the first teacher of the French program at my school and my language colleague was only hired part-time, I did not exactly start with a strong language team. My grade level team became my family. We ate lunch together, planned English together, made rush copies for each other, organized grade-level field trips, celebrated each other's successes, birthdays, and children, etc. I was able to borrow their beginning of the year activities and translated them into French. We discussed math instruction and figured out the best way to teach numbers, addition, and subtraction. We talked about writing expectations and reading strategies. We heavily discussed homework packets; I went rogue to be the only teacher who did not have packets. In my own defense, my students were required to read for 20 minutes every day, practice typing or coding, listen to the song of the week, and watch my flipped classroom videos on letter writing. This said, due to our constant collaboration, our classrooms looked very similar even though we taught in four different languages. We had our own flair with each language, but it was obvious to any visitor that we worked together as a team. Having a united front with your grade level team is important, not only for horizontal alignment purposes, but it also decreases the teacher jealousy, school politics, and parent comments of "I want my child to be in Ms. A's class because she does XYZ."

Once my French team started growing, I spent time with my language colleagues after school for long-term vision planning. We were lucky and had a few days of language planning that our principal had organized. Nevertheless, we still used a lot of our own time. During these planning meetings, we talked about our translations of normal protocols that were commonly used in class (e.g. Kagan strategies and graphic organizers), grade level writing expectations (e.g. specific sentence frames), themes and books we loved using, grant money use, cultural events, etc. It was important to me that the first grade teacher knew the exact sentence frames I was teaching throughout the year so that I would not hear, "Why was __ not taught in kindergarten?" The vertical alignment we had created as our program grew also built-in grade-level accountability. Each teacher knew the sight words, sentence frames, reading comprehension competence, etc. for which we were responsible. No teacher could make another feel bad about not covering an important aspect of our instructional language that we felt needed to be done in the previous grade level. Using the same translation of strategies and graphic organizers also ensured our students were not confused from one class to the next. Furthermore, despite having different teaching styles, the parents in the program saw continuity in language development from one teacher to another. While not every teacher on my language team was my best friend, we worked together attentively to be on the same page for our students. You can be sure that I am proud of the program we created and the linguistic progress the kiddos have made. In 2018, our French program was the first California school to receive the international accreditation, Label FrancEducation, awarded by the French Ministry of Foreign Affairs.[40]

Another reason your grade level and language partners are going to be super important to you and your development in the program is campus and district politics. I hate to say it, but it is true. Education is a political place. Depending on your period of hiring and the district's intention for growth of your dual immersion program, there may be tension among the English teachers. The growth of the program you are in may have pushed out beloved English-only teachers who are an institution at the school. It is not your personal fault, per se, but the tension is there. The school that I was at was in the middle of this transition and the morale in certain areas of the school was extremely low. Our staff meetings may not have always been the happiest with teachers knowing that they were going to be leaving at one time or another. It was never an overt dislike, because they did welcome me and help me when needed, but I did not feel the warmth. Does that make sense? My grade level and language teams were the ones who raised my spirits and helped me feel at home because I knew that they wanted me there. They also understood the feeling and the mood of the school. Furthermore, we knew that we were going to be the future "institutions" of our school.

---

[40] Label FrancEducation: frenchlanguagek12.org/dual-language/FranceEducation

All of this to say, you should not and do not have to work and teach alone. Spend time with your colleagues, especially those from your grade level and language team so that you can ensure horizontal and vertical alignment. If they are not available to you because you are the only person in your program right now, find your group on social media. I will happily be a part of your group, too!

Please do not work alone. You are supported and you do not need to reinvent the wheel. Working in a team and sharing with others is so important to our sanity as dual immersion teachers. You can do this. I believe in you. You've got this!

Your Cheerleader,

Valerie

LETTER 13 CHECKLIST

- ☐ Meet with your language team to discuss vertical alignment and articulation.
- ☐ Find time to be with your grade level or language teams outside of work - for fun - at least once a year.
- ☐ Search for a Professional Learning Community or Network (PLC or PLN) based on your instructional language or teaching interest. NABE and ACTFL are good places to start your search for local affiliates.
- ☐ If you are currently not on social media, create an account that will be only for professional use. Twitter is a good place to start.
- ☐ Follow Valerie on Twitter - @MlleValSunshine or @EmpowerED_PD, if you would like!

LETTER 14: STUDENTS WITH SPECIAL NEEDS

Dear Dual Immersion Teacher,

If your class is representative of a typical class, even in dual immersion, you will have at least one student with special needs. The student's needs may vary from requiring small modifications to having a full-time shadow in your class. I would like to make a clear stance and state that students with special needs deserve to be in dual immersion programs and we need to make sure that these students are receiving the necessary support to succeed.

As teachers, we are on the front lines and having a kiddo with special needs may render our classroom lives a little haywire. Nevertheless, they make us better teachers and we need to advocate for them. There are multiple studies by Fred Genesee[41] and Tara Fortune,[42] among other researchers who have followed students with special needs who remained or were pushed out of dual immersion programs. They remarked that these struggling students in dual immersion also had the same difficulties (behavior, language development, and/or academics) in English-only programs. Thus, for the students who have learning disabilities and/or special needs, it made more sense for them to at least have the advantage of being bilingual and biliterate.

So, how does this translate to practice in your class? Advocacy, patience, and support from the parents and administrators. As a kindergarten teacher, less than a handful of students came in with an IEP. I was immediately in contact with the parents whose students

---

[41] Genesee, F. (2007). French immersion and at-risk students: A review of research evidence. *The Canadian Modern Language Review.* 63 (5), 655-688

[42] Genesee, F. and Fortune, T.W. (2014). Bilingual education and at-risk students. *Journal of Immersion and content-based language education,* 2(2), 196-209

had files. There were some students who did not arrive in kindergarten with prior diagnoses who needed additional help. It was a long journey to receive the assistance. The craziest part of all of this was that parents have almost all the power in this situation. As I mentioned in previous letters, parent voices in advocacy will be much more useful than yours. Hence, that phone call at the beginning of the school year where you established a positive relationship is extremely important. There are parents who will refuse to believe that their child needs extra assistance and support. Be understanding of their perspective: It is a hard reality to accept that your own child is different in a society where special needs is negatively labeled. There are also parents who will underestimate the ability of their child and will feel burdensome to you as a teacher for not providing every support the parents deem necessary. In both cases, understand the parents' perspective, the fear that drives them to act and react, and be their partner. It is only through a positive partnership that you can have an aligned front to provide the most supportive learning environment for the student. It is important to stay focused on the developmental needs of the student. This is about the child, not your ego, nor the guardians' parenting skills.

To be clear, you are a teacher, and you cannot diagnose a student with a learning disorder. You can communicate with parents about the extra support you have put in place that has been necessary for their child to succeed. You can encourage parents to speak to the child's pediatrician regarding your concerns and provide examples of the support that you use in class to receive a medical evaluation. You can document the student's behavior in class through an objective lens. Nevertheless, no matter the years of experience you have as a teacher, you cannot tell a parent a diagnosis of their child. Let me say it again: You are a teacher, and you cannot diagnose a child with a learning disorder. Got it? Good.

I had a student, Jake, who kept confusing colors when we were working on color identification. He was a native speaker and a smart kiddo who worked well in all other aspects. I suspected colorblindness, but I was (and still am not) a medical doctor thus I could not diagnose him nor share my suspicions of a possible diagnosis. After a few more days of witnessing Jake's struggles, I mentioned the incidents to his mother after school when all the other parents had left. I asked her if she had noticed anything at home. She thought for a while and said she had not paid attention to notice, but she would. She also said that it had been a while since his last eye exam and said maybe she should make an appointment. So, I encouraged her to complete color identification activities with her child and to make an appointment with the pediatrician. Never, in any of the interactions did I mention colorblindness to her. I stated my observations objectively and encouraged her when she suggested an appointment. It is important that you stay objective in this matter and do not state your opinions.

While colorblindness is not a disruptive issue to have in the classroom, there are other cases where behavior and learning disabilities are more complex and need more support. The most important part is to document the incidents, create a Student Success Team (SST), and inform the parents so that you can form a united front to have the most appropriate support for the student. If it is a serious behavior disruption, it is imperative that you inform the office to receive administrative help. Be sure to document the behavior after debriefing with your administrative team and inform the student's parents. There had been times when I knew the office was going to call home or had already called the parents, but I still called the parents anyway. It was my way of informing them that we are on the same team and want the best for the child. This way, we could also be on the same page in terms of consequences and action plan for the next steps.

Working with students with special needs is not easy. I have had students who were outwardly violent where evacuation drills were necessary, students who had a hard time with letter identification even at the end of kindergarten, students on the Autism spectrum who needed extra attention, and some with speech impediments. I have had fleeting moments when I felt that maybe dual immersion was not the best environment for the child's social, emotional, and academic development. Just as it was not my place to diagnose a child, it was also not my place to decide if a child should stay in the program. In those moments, I would remind myself of the bigger picture - an opportunity to learn a second language as an advantage to their situation - and the research conducted by Genesee, Fortune, among others stating that students with special needs *do* belong in dual immersion programs.

Your job as a dual immersion teacher is to try your best to work with the parents and administrators so that you have a united front to provide the best support for the student to learn the language and the content. You will also let parents know that learning supports do not stop after the school day. As a teacher, I recommended games, activities, and sometimes consequences so that there would be follow through with the actions taken at school and in the classroom.

It is often hard to support students with special needs in dual immersion and it takes a whole team to do it. Talk to your administrators about the support that you need. Document your requests in a follow-up email so there is a trail demonstrating your initiative. Inform the parents of the support that is necessary so that you can both advocate for change. One way or another, remember that students with special needs have a place in dual immersion. With the appropriate support in place, they will succeed. Believe in the best in the child. You are capable. You are doing the best that you can. I believe in you. You've got this!

Your Cheerleader,

Valerie

LETTER 14 CHECKLIST

☐ Look over your student roster to see if there are students with special needs in your class.

☐ Reach out to the parents to understand the successful supports that were in place last year and the systems they have at home.

☐ Get a notebook or create a digital document to record your observations. Stay objective.

☐ Talk to the special education teacher or support provider on your campus to learn strategies you can use.

☐ When necessary, speak to your administrator.

Valerie Sun

LETTER 15: END OF THE YEAR

Dear Dual Immersion Teacher,

You are an absolute rockstar. You did it! You have made it to the end of the school year. Hopefully, this will be your first with many more to come. You are amazing. I hope you are relishing in the language and cultural growth of your students and have beautiful memories of the productive struggles that your students experienced and conquered. I also hope that you can take some time to reflect on the professional journey that you have accomplished. Honestly, I worked so hard and so much during my very first year, approximately 17-18 hours each day, even on the weekends, that I could not see the forest for the trees. I was also ready to go on a serious vacation as soon as the school year was over. The same day after saying goodbye to my students, I packed up the technology tools that needed to be locked up in the school office and checked out of my classroom with my principal. I was on a flight to France for a six-week vacation the following afternoon.

Back to finishing the school year. Plan at least a 30-minute block of time to check-in with your students. What were some units and projects that they really enjoyed? What was their favorite book? If you completed any of the first day of school and beginning of the year activities, take them out from their boxes, return them, and have a reflection moment with your students. Let your students write to the next class and provide insight to their learning. If you are a techy teacher and recorded your students throughout the year, collectively listen to their compiled works from the beginning of the school year. Show them the linguistic and cultural growth that they have made and celebrate their successes! It is hard for students to see their own incremental progress at times, and truthfully, you also deserve a celebration for the growth you have helped them develop.

I always got emotional fastening the last students' memory book in preparation for the end of the year. Our class memory book was compiled with selected works completed during the 10 months of the school year. Each month contained a calendar that students wrote and colored, one art activity that they created, one piece of writing from the end of the month, and one photo from an event we had in class or at school. It is hard putting together the entire memory book at the end of the school year. However, if you have parent helpers during the year to help you glue pages or photos on construction paper, it becomes a lot easier to put them together at the end. While compiling and fastening the memory book, I would witness the learning journey of each student and the crazy amount of work we had put in together. I called these kids my kinder babies because after spending 180 days with them, they felt like my own kids. They defined my work, my being, and my passion. I learned from them just as much as they have learned from me throughout the year. Together, we also built a strong culture of love and support. I knew every year that I had prepared them well for the next school year and that they would come back to visit me in my classroom. I also used this moment to cry so that I would not fall apart in front of them on the last day of school.

At my school, we did not have a promotion ceremony for kindergarten to first grade. However, I made this momentous day into an event in my class and to complete a full circle. On the first day of kindergarten, every child went home wearing a "I survived my first day of Kindergarten!" crown that they decorated and had written their name. So, on the last day of school, my students also designed the same crowns, but this time with the words "I'm going to First Grade!" The parents came in around 45 minutes before the end of the day. We would put on an in-class show with the students' favorite songs and dances. I would have the opportunity to recognize the parents who consistently helped me throughout the year with a thoughtful gift. Two sample class gifts that I have offered to the parent helpers were a thyme plant in student-decorated and signed pots with the note, "merci beaucoup pour votre *thym* dans la classe!"

and oven mitts that all students had signed with the message, "vous nous chauffez le coeur avec votre assistance pendant l'année." Lastly, we finished the day by calling up each student and I helped staple and put on their crowns. The students loved the show and felt proud of their accomplishments even with a simple ceremony, the parents felt validated in getting to celebrate their students, and I enjoyed having the opportunity to say thank you and goodbye to each family. The event was a good way to close out the school year.

With my students' feedback, I also reflected a lot regarding the activities we completed together. There were some things that I would probably never attempt again (e.g. going to the art museum where each student had a clipboard to draw - museum, yes; clipboard, no), and others have become classics that I would feel remiss to not complete with my class (e.g. city planning after learning about community helpers). It is important for you to go through this reflection process so that you can better plan for next year. Furthermore, look at your end-of-year assessment data. Did most of your students reach their grade level standards that were set? If not, you will need to disaggregate the data to find the reason(s). Was there something that was not scaffolded enough? Was it an issue with content vocabulary? Finding the answers to your questions will help guide your backwards planning to help your students reach their grade level goals next year. If this is an issue with vertical alignment, then you will need to meet with your language team to determine a plan for more continuity in scaffolding within the language across the grade levels. Find time to work with your language partners over the summer and ask your principal to be compensated for your time. You will need to come up with a plan so that each grade level teacher is aware of the language development and sentence frames necessary to meet their grade level standards.

As much as language and content are important to develop in dual immersion teaching, students are not going to remember the exact worksheet or activity that you completed together. It will be the way you taught them, made them feel, and encouraged their curiosity for the language that will carry on. How do you think your students will remember you as their teacher?

Thank you for jumping in this grand adventure as a dual immersion teacher and continuing to share the love of your language and culture with the students. Here is to many more years in dual immersion. I promise that next school year will be a lot better, you will feel more confident, and you will continue to be the rockstar teacher that you are. I believe in you. You've got this!

Your Cheerleader,

Valerie

Ps. Please find some time to rest over the summer. You deserve it!

LETTER 15 CHECKLIST

- ☐ Review your end-of-year assessment data.
- ☐ Celebrate your students' accomplishments.
- ☐ Let yourself feel the accomplishment you achieved.
- ☐ Plan for time to be away from your work.
- ☐ When you are ready, plan with your language partners for vertical alignment.
- ☐ Optional: Cry with happiness.

ABOUT THE AUTHOR

Valerie Sun, Ed.D. is a multilingual/multicultural techy educator and a firm believer that everyone should have access to learning a second language at a young age. As the pioneering French dual immersion teacher in Glendale, California, she created the kindergarten curriculum and worked together with incoming colleagues to develop a strong vertical alignment. She continues to support dual immersion and world language teachers in Glendale and other schools and districts. She teaches courses at CSU, Los Angeles, CSU East Bay, and with the California World Language Project at Occidental College focusing on instructional practices with educational technology in dual immersion classrooms. Dr. Sun provides professional development for educators and fosters collaboration among dual immersion stakeholders through EmpowerED Consulting, a non-profit organization she founded.

ABOUT TBR BOOKS

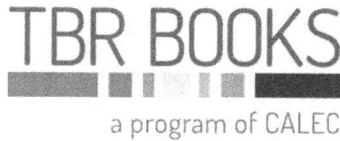

TBR BOOKS

a program of CALEC

TBR Books is a program of the Center for the Advancement of Languages, Education, and Communities. We publish researchers and practitioners who seek to engage diverse communities on topics related to education, languages, cultural history, and social initiatives. We translate our books in a variety of languages to further expand our impact.

📖 BOOKS IN ENGLISH AND OTHER LANGUAGES

Navigating Dual Immersion: A Teacher's Companion for the School Year and Beyond by Valerie Sun

One Good Question: How to Ask Challenging Questions that Lead You to Real Solutions by Rhonda Broussard

Bilingual Children: Families, Education, and Development by Ellen Bialystok

Can We Agree to Disagree? by Sabine Landolt and Agathe Laurent

Salsa Dancing in Gym Shoes by Tammy Oberg de la Garza and Alyson Leah Lavigne

Beyond Gibraltar; The Other Shore; Mamma in her Village by Maristella de Panizza Lorch

The Clarks of Willsborough Point by Darcey Hale

The English Patchwork by Pedro Tozzi and Giovanna de Lima

Two Centuries of French Education in New York: The Role of Schools in Cultural Diplomacy by Jane Flatau Ross

The Bilingual Revolution: The Future of Education is in Two Languages by Fabrice Jaumont

BOOKS IN FRENCH

Deux siècles d'enseignement français à New York : le rôle des écoles dans la diplomatie culturelle by Jane Flatau Ross

Sénégalais de l'étranger by Maya Smith

Le projet Colibri : créer à partir de "rien" by Vickie Frémont

Pareils mais différents : une exploration des différences entre les Américains et les Français au travail by Sabine Landolt and Agathe Laurent

Le don des langues : vers un changement de paradigme dans l'enseignement des langues aux USA by Fabrice Jaumont and Kathleen Stein-Smith

BILINGUAL EDITIONS

Peshtigo 1871 by Charles Mercier

The Word of the Month by Ben Lévy, Jim Sheppard and Andrew Arnon

BOOKS FOR CHILDREN (available in several languages)

Rainbows, Masks, and Ice Cream by Deana Sobel Lederman

Korean Super New Years with Grandma by Mary Chi-Whi Kim and Eunjoo Feaster

Math for All by Mark Hansen

Rose Alone by Sheila Decosse

Uncle Steve's Country Home; The Blue Dress; The Good, the Ugly, and the Great by Teboho Moja

Immunity Fun!; Respiratory Fun!; Digestive Fun! By Dounia Stewart-McMeel

Marimba by Christine Hélot, Patricia Velasco, Antun Kojton

Our books are available on our website and on all major online bookstores as paperback and e-book. Some of our books have been translated in over a dozen languages. For a listing of all books published by TBR Books, information on our series, or for our submission guidelines for authors, visit our website at:

www.tbr-books.o

The Center for the Advancement of Languages, Education, and Communities (CALEC) is a nonprofit organization focused on promoting multilingualism, empowering multilingual families, and fostering cross-cultural understanding. The Center's mission is in alignment with the United Nations' Sustainable Development Goals. Our mission is to establish language as a critical life skill, through developing and implementing bilingual education programs, promoting diversity, reducing inequality, and helping to provide quality education. Our programs seek to protect world cultural heritage and support teachers, authors, and families by providing the knowledge and resources to create vibrant multilingual communities.

The specific objectives and purpose of our organization are:

- To develop and implement education programs that promote multilingualism and cross-cultural understanding, and establish an inclusive and equitable quality education, including internship and leadership training. [SDG # 4, Quality Education]

- To publish and distribute resources, including research papers, books, and case studies that seek to empower and promote the social, economic, and political inclusion of all, with a focus on language education and cultural diversity, equity, and inclusion. [SDG # 10, Reduced Inequalities]

- To help build sustainable cities and communities and support teachers, authors, researchers, and families in the advancement of multilingualism and cross-cultural understanding through collaborative tools for linguistic communities. [SDG # 11, Sustainable Cities and Communities]

- To foster strong global partnerships and cooperation, and mobilize resources across borders, to participate in events and activities that promote language education through knowledge sharing and coaching, empowering parents, and teachers, and building multilingual societies. [SDG # 17, Partnerships for the Goals]

SOME GOOD REASONS TO SUPPORT US

Your donation helps:

- develop our publishing and translation activities so that more languages are represented.
- provide access to our online book platform to daycare centers, schools, and cultural centers in underserved areas.
- support local and sustainable action in favor of education and multilingualism.
- implement projects that advance dual-language education
- organize workshops for parents, conferences with large audiences, meet-the-author chats, and talks with experts in multilingualism.

DONATE ONLINE

For all your questions, contact our team by email at contact@calec.org or donate online on our website:

www.calec.org

www.ingramcontent.com/pod-product-compliance
Lightning Source LLC
Chambersburg PA
CBHW070046100426
42740CB00013B/2824